KANAE INOUE

# REAL BENTO

## FRESH AND EASY LUNCHBOX RECIPES
## FROM A JAPANESE WORKING MOM

TUTTLE Publishing

Tokyo │ Rutland, Vermont │ Singapore

# Contents

## Simple Salt and Pepper

Chicken & Pepper Stir-Fry  34
Grilled Sweet Potato  34
Salt & Sesame Cabbage  34
Herb-Grilled Lotus Root  34
Crunchy Chicken Patties  35
Celery with Sesame  35
Simple Sautéed Chicken  35
Sesame Pork with Pea Shoots  35
Salted Salmon  36
Sesame Bell Peppers  36
Japanese-Style Broccoli  36
Grilled Onions  36
Spicy Potato and Carrot  37
Steamed Eggplant  37
Tofu Fritters  37
Mini Pork Patties  37

## Seasoned with Miso

Pork and Eggplant Rolls  38
Chicken in Miso Sauce  38
Spinach with Sesame-Miso  38
Miso Potatoes  38
Chicken with Sweet Miso  39
Cabbage with Mustard-Miso Mayo  39
Cheese and Tofu Rolls  39
Lotus Root and Chicken with Miso  39
Chicken with Miso Mayo  40
Pork & Peppers with Miso  40
Carrot with Miso Sauce  40
Pumpkin with Miso Butter  40

Grilled Onions with Miso Mayo  41
Eggplant with Plum Miso  41
Broccoli and Pasta Miso Salad  41
Creamy Miso Potatoes  41

## Seasoned with Soy Sauce

Pork and Celery Noodles  42
Pork with Mustard-Soy Sauce  42
Salmon and Green Beans in Soy Sauce  42
Fish Sticks with Cheese  42
Cheese & Cabbage Rolls  43
Savory Cabbage  43
Mustard-Soy Chicken  43
Tofu Steaks with Soy Sauce  43
Speedy Noodle Stir-Fry  44
Spinach & Ginger Tofu  44
Spicy Eggplant  44
Pumpkin with Soy Sauce  44
Pork & Eggplant Soboro  45
Seafood in Soy Sauce  45
Savory Carrot Pancakes  45
Spicy Pea Shoots and Cheese  45

## Seasoned with Mayo

Mackerel with Mayo  46
Mayo Pork & Mushrooms  46
Spicy Mayo Cabbage  46
Tangy Carrot Salad  46
Mini Omelets  47
Broccoli with Sesame Mayo  47
Oyster Sauce Chicken  47
Noodles with Soy Sauce and Mayo  47
Chicken with Mayo and Citrus Sauce  48
Burdock Root Salad  48
Celery and Egg Salad  48
Sautéed Salmon & Mayo  48
Pumpkin and Bacon Salad  49
Miso-Mayo Eggplant  49
Seafood and Mushroom Stir-Fry  49
Tangy Potato Salad  49

## Seasoned with Tomato Ketchup

Savory Pork and Onions  50
Teriyaki Salmon  50
Crunchy Lotus Root  50
Cheesy Ketchup Pumpkin  50
Chopped Pork Patties  50
Chili Chicken  50
Fluffy Egg with Ketchup  51
Stir-Fried Beef  51
Mushrooms with Ketchup  51
Tofu with Ketchup  51
Chicken & Green Beans  51
Cabbage Omelet  51

## Seasoned with Pickled Plum

Chicken in Plum Sauce  52
Zingy Spinach & Cheese  52

Plum & Soy Mackerel  52
Cabbage & Plum Salad  52
Chicken Piccata  52
Zesty Chicken Sauté  52
Chicken & Plum patties  53
Omelet with Plum  53
Potato Namul with Plum  53
Eggplant in Plum Sauce  53
Stir-Fried Plum Noodles  53
Cheesy Pork Rolls  53

## Seasoned with Curry

Curried Grilled Salmon  54
Buttery Spinach & Corn  54
Curried Pork with Green Beans  54
Stir-Fried Curried Pork  54
Curry-Marinated Carrot  54
Honey Teriyaki Chicken  54
Curried Chicken  55
Spicy Buttered Pumpkin  55
Curried Onion Tempura  55
Crispy Curried Chicken  55
Curried Noodles  55
Curried Cheese Omelet  55

## Salads and Sweet Touches

Stir-Fried Seafood  56
Sweet Orange and Tomato  56
Marinated Strawberries  56
Kiwi and Carrot Salad  56
Potato and Apple Salad  57
Grapefruit and Celery Salad  57
Crunchy Coleslaw  57
"Sweet" Potato Salad  57
Apple & Cabbage Salad  57
Honey Nut Squash Salad  57

# CHAPTER 2

# Time-Saving Techniques

CHAPTER 3

# Tips for Good-Looking Bentos

# Meet the Family

## Kanae (me)

I love cooking and make a living as a cook and food blogger. I go to Tokyo as often as eight times a month for work, but try to come home on the same day. The reason? To make bentos for my family. No matter how late I get home, or even on days when I have a hangover, I always get up at five thirty every morning to make bentos.

## Tenkichi (our son)

A sophomore in college. Even though he can eat anything he wants really cheaply at the school cafeteria or at any number of restaurants elsewhere, for some reason he brings a bento with him from home every day . . . maybe he's trying to save money? Incidentally he's a good cook - good enough to impress his sisters when mom is away on a business trip!

## Naa (our older daughter)

In the third year of middle school, she has to take a bento to school for lunch every day. There is a school cafeteria, but the after-school sports club she belongs to forbids her from eating there, and also requires her to keep her weight in check. She loves eating above all else. She loves Thai food, fresh coriander, oysters . . . she's always thinking about food.

## Sue (our younger daughter)

In the first year of middle school. Her school has a lunch program, so she basically doesn't need to bring bentos, but she does occasionally need bentos on the weekends for her club activities or for school outings and events. She is a very picky eater, with definite likes and dislikes, so her mother is already worried about what's going to happen if she has to bring a bento every day once she gets to high school.

## Hubby (my husband)

A businessman, six years older than me. Even though his wife is getting rather well known in the food world, he has a policy of not talking about her work at all to his work colleagues, friends or other acquaintances. Previously, not only could he not cook, he never even entered the kitchen! But recently he has developed the ability to make coffee. This is a dramatic improvement.

## Mei (our beloved dog)

A girl labrador retriever. She loves Mom to bits, and stalks her all the time.

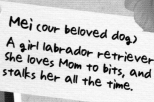

# My Bento Philosophy

About ten years after I put my oldest son in daycare and went back to work, I started making bento lunches for my husband and myself. That was when I published my first book of hearty, simple bentos filled with the brown-colored food that my husband loves, titled *Bentos for Guys*. So I was making "guy bentos" for my husband, and then for my son too, once he started middle school and had soccer club every weekend. Since then, five years have passed. My oldest daughter has started middle school, and now I'm in the throes of making bentos without a break seven days a week, with my daughter's taking center stage. She needs bentos every day, and my oldest son, who's now in college, needs a bento four days a week. (Incidentally, my husband now has his lunches at his company cafeteria, which are delicious.)

Unlike the "guy bentos" I started out making, the bentos I make for my two daughters, who are much more critical, are first and foremost ones that make them happy, or what I like to call "praiseworthy bentos." From my point of view, as the bento chef of the family, they also must be:

- easy and quick to make, using inexpensive ingredients

- really delicious, nice to look at, and something my daughters will want to show off to their friends

My older daughter in particular always gives me feedback, really focusing on the flavor of every item I put into her bentos. Based on what she tells me, I get to thinking, "Well, next time I'll try this," or "Tomorrow I'm going to make her a bento that makes her even happier," or "She'll love it if I put that in her bento tomorrow." And that, I think, is the reason why my bento making has improved — or perhaps I should say, continues to improve!

In this, my ultimate bento book, I have put together bento items that can be made using various time-saving tricks in ten minutes in the morning, using basic ingredients found in any ordinary refrigerator. On top of that, I try to make bentos that will make demanding teenage girls in middle and high school squeal "Delicous! Cute! You're the best, Mom!" I really hope that this book will help you, the reader, make praiseworthy, everyday bentos too!

# Basic Ingredients for Bentos

Most of the ingredients I use all the time are those that are available year round, at any supermarket. Even though the ingredients are nothing special and easy to get hold of, I can still make delicious, varied and great-looking bento lunch boxes that my kids love.

You'll also find recipes in this book that make use of Japanese ingredients you may be less familiar with. Where possible, Western ingredients are given as substitutes, but if you can get hold of the Japanese ingredients, why not give them a try? Many of them are starting to become widely available in regular supermarkets and you can also find them at your nearest Japanese grocery store, or online.

The ingredient notes on these pages are divided into Bento Staples and Japanese and Other Asian Ingredients. If your kitchen is stocked with the items on the list of Bento Staples you'll have more than enough for your bento-making needs. The Japanese and other Asian ingredients or their recommended substitutes will add a delicious, authentic flavor, and make your kids the envy of their classmates!

## Bento Staples

### Aromatic vegetables
I like to make use of green onions (scallions), baby leeks or fat green onions, and ginger. A little of any of these goes a long way to adding flavor and fragrance to a dish.

### Bacon
The salty, rich taste of bacon is a great addition to a bento-box lunch.

### Bell peppers
Great for adding crunch and color to stir-fries. I use both the immature green type and the ripe red or yellow peppers.

### Bottled lemon juice
Handy to have for those times when you don't have fresh lemon juice. Perks up dishes with a fresh, sour note.

### Broccoli
Colorful and cute, broccoli adds visual appeal and is also packed with nutrients.

### Butter
The butter used in this book is salted.

### Cabbage
Cabbage is widely used in both Western and Japanese dishes. It's a versatile ingredient that can be cooked in lots of different ways.

### Carrots
Carrots keep well, are very nutritious and make your bentos more colorful!

### Canned fish
I always have a stock of canned tuna, mackerel, etc., for quick and nutritious side dishes or salads.

### Celery
This is my family's favorite vegetable. The flavor and fragrance are addictive!

### Cheese
I use sliced processed cheese, cream cheese and grated cheese to add flavor and richness.

### Chicken
Use boneless chicken thighs, breast meat or tenders depending on your preferences and the recipe.

### Eggplant
This is also a favorite vegetable in my family—my daughter Naa loves them! Japanese eggplants are much smaller than European or American types. You can find small Japanese eggplants at Japanese grocery stores, or slim Chinese ones at general Asian or Chinese stores. The recipes in this book will work with any kind of eggplant, including the larger type most commonly available in the West.

### Eggs

Eggs are star ingredients in bentos; they score high in the flavor, looks and nutritional-value categories.

### Frozen seafood mix

If I don't have any fresh fish on hand, this frozen staple can save the day.

### Green beans

Thin and easy to handle. For the same reason, asparagus and sugar snap peas are also good bento staples.

### Green leafy vegetables

I use spinach, bok choy, pea sprouts, etc. For an Asian twist, try a Japanese leafy green such as komatsuna. Several recipes in this book call for blanched, squeezed-out spinach. To blanch spinach or similar leafy greens, bring a pot of water to a boil, add the greens and cook for a couple of minutes. Drain and cool rapidly under cold running water. Drain again when cooled, and tightly squeeze out excess moisture.

### Ground meat

I use beef, chicken, pork or a mix of half beef and half pork depending on the recipe.

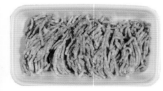

### Italian herb mix

A quick and easy way to vary the flavor of a dish.

### Maple syrup

A useful source of sweetness in liquid form. It has a milder flavor than honey.

### Mayonnaise

Japanese mayonnaise, such as the Kewpie brand, has a sweeter, more eggy flavor than most North American or European brands, but you can use your favorite mayonnaise without any issues. In Japan mayonnaise is often used for cooking with, not just in salads and sandwiches. Japanese mayonnaise brands like Kewpie are available at Japanese grocery stores.

### Nuts and dried fruit

I use almonds, raisins, etc., to add texture and variety to salads.

### Oily fish

Fish such as mackerel has lots of beneficial oils and is rich in flavor.

### Onions

Onions are another good keeper. Versatile and useful, they can be the stars or the supporting players in any bento. *See also* Ready-made fried onions.

### Oyster sauce

A Chinese sauce made from oysters. It has a rich, dark color and strong flavor.

### Potatoes

Potatoes keep well and are filling too, so they're very useful to have on hand.

### Rice

The rice used throughout this book is white medium grain or Japonica-type rice that is steam-cooked in a pot or rice cooker. This is the rice all the recipes in this book were designed to match well with, but you can use any other grain of your choice.

### Ready-made fried onions

These can be used instead of sautéed onions, or to add depth of flavor to dishes. *See also* Onions.

### Thinly sliced meat

Used for stir-fries and vegetable-meat rolls. I use pork, chicken thighs and beef. (If you can't find thin slices like this at your local supermarket, freeze a block of meat for an hour and slice it thinly with a sharp knife.)

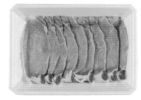

### White fish

Fish such as cod and salmon (yes, salmon is classified as a white fish!) are light in flavor and can take on all kinds of other flavors.

# Japanese and Other Asian Ingredients

### Abura-age tofu

Abura-age is a deep-fried tofu pouch, available at Japanese grocery stores. A deep fried tofu product often called "tofu puffs", available at general Asian or Chinese grocery stores, can be substituted in recipes that call for abura-age.

### Aonori seaweed powder

This is a versatile ingredient that adds color and variety. Available at Japanese grocery stores or online. Use crazy salt if you can't get hold of aonori.

### Beni shoga red pickled ginger

Young ginger that has been pickled in a salty-sour pickling liquid. The color varies from bright red to purple-pink, depending on the type of coloring agent used. Available at Japanese or general Asian grocery stores. Don't confuse with gari, the pale pink pickled ginger eaten with sushi.

### Bonito flakes

Called katsuobushi in Japanese, these are flakes of fermented, dried and aged skipjack tuna or bonito. It is an essential ingredient in Japanese cooking, used to make dashi or Japanese stock, and also as a garnish or topping. The size of the flakes ranges from very fine and powder-like to large, long shavings that look like wood shavings. Use in bentos to add an instant shot of umami, as well as to soak up excess moisture. Available at Japanese grocery stores or online.

### Burdock root

The distinctive crunchy texture and earthy flavor really whet the appetite. You can find burdock root for sale at East Asian grocery stores. If you can't find burdock root, carrot has a similar texture.

### Chikuwa fish sticks

These can be eaten as-is or stir-fried. I often use them as a substitute for squid in recipes. You can find chikuwa fish sticks at Japanese grocery stores. In many recipes you can substitute frankfurters, wiener sausages or boneless chicken.

### Chinese noodles

Chinese wheat noodles that are used for stir-fried noodles dishes are usually sold in Chinese or general Asian stores uncooked, but in Japan they are usually sold pre-steamed and ready to stir-fry. You can find the pre-steamed type of noodle in Japanese grocery stores sold as "yakisoba noodles", but if you can't get them you can use fresh uncooked Chinese noodles. Just boil them briefly, drain well, rinse under running water, drain well again, and use in stir-fried dishes.

### Daikon radish

This is a thick white root vegetable with a spicy flavor and a crunchy texture when raw. Cooked, it becomes soft and sweet. You can find it at Asian grocery stores as well at many regular supermarkets.

### Doubanjiang chili bean paste

A fermented, very hot and spicy paste from Sichuan province in China, made with fava (broad) beans, soy beans, salt, rice and spices. It is used to add heat and umami to various dishes. In Japanese it's called tobanjan. A little goes a long way. Available at general Asian or Japanese grocery stores.

### Dried, cut wakame seaweed

See Wakame seaweed.

### Dried sakura shrimp

See Sakura shrimp.

### Freeze-dried tofu

Freeze dried tofu, called koya dofu in Japanese, is very healthy like regular tofu, but is surprisingly filling because of the slightly meaty, spongy texture. Available at Japanese grocery stores or online.

### Glass noodles

Also known as cellophane noodles. These are made with various types of starch, such as potato or sweet-potato starch, or mung bean starch. The type most commonly used in Japanese cooking is called harusame (which means "spring rain") and is made from potato starch. Glass noodles are always sold in dried form, and are available at general Asian grocery stores.

### Gochujang bean paste

A spicy fermented paste from Korea that's made with chili, rice, soybeans and barley. It adds spiciness as well as a little sweetness, and is not as hot as Chinese doubanjiang chili bean paste. Available in tubes or tubs at Korean or Japanese grocery stores.

## Japanese seven spice

Called shichimi togarashi or naname togarashi in Japanese, this is a spice mix with seven different dried ingredients, including red chili pepper, citrus peel, sesame seeds and poppy seeds. The formula varies with the brand. Available at Japanese, general Asian and some general supermarkets as well as online.

## Kabocha squash

Sweet enough to be a dessert. The dark green skin is edible and looks great in a bento next to the orange flesh of the kabocha. Butternut squash can be used as a substitute.

## Karashi mustard

This hot, yellow mustard is similar to English mustard, which can be used as a substitute in the recipes in this book. "Oriental hot mustard," available in regular supermarkets, can also be used. Karashi mustard can be found in Japanese groceries, in powdered form or ready-made in a tube.

## Koya dofu

See Freeze-dried tofu.

## Lotus root

A great bento vegetable that scores high in the looks department. The texture changes depending on how it's cut. You can find lotus root for sale at East Asian grocery stores.

## Mentsuyu sauce

This is a bottled sauce made with soy sauce, mirin, sake, sugar and dashi stock. It is usually sold as a concentrate that is diluted with water to make a noodle sauce, but is popular as a cooking ingredient too. A double-concentrate type of mentsuyu is used throughout this book. Check the concentration on the bottle you have and adjust the recipe accordingly. A 3x concentrate type will be saltier straight out of the bottle than a 2x concentrate. You can find mentsuyu at Japanese grocery stores, and it is becoming more widely available in regular supermarkets. Kikkoman also sell a mentsuyu-like product called Memmi, which is available in Western supermarkets. If you are unable to find mentsuyu or Memmi, add a little soy sauce to the recipe instead.

## Mirin

Mirin, also called hon mirin, is a sweet alcoholic liquor made from rice. Although it is a beverage, nowadays it's used almost exclusively for cooking. It has a sweet taste and is often used instead of sugar in various recipes, and is a staple in Japanese kitchens. You can also find something called mirin seasoning or aji mirin, which is an alcohol-free substitute for mirin that contains sweeteners (sugar or high-fructose corn syrup), salt and monosodium glutamate. Mirin seasoning will do in a pinch, but real mirin has a better flavor. Available at Japanese and general Asian grocery stores as well as some general supermarkets.

## Miso

Miso is a fermented paste made with soy beans, salt, and Aspergillus oryzae microbes. Grains such as wheat, rice or barley are often added to the mix before fermenting. The color of miso can range from a pale yellow-brown to a deep-reddish brown, almost black. Miso can be found at many regular supermarkets and health food stores as well as at Japanese groceries.

## Nori seaweed

Seaweed or laver that is stretched out in sheets and dried. The best nori has a green-black color. This is the seaweed that's wrapped around sushi rolls. It's available in many regular supermarkets as well as in Japanese grocery stores.

## Okonomiyaki sauce

Used on the Japanese savory pancakes called okonomiyaki, this is a variant of tonkatsu sauce (see page 14), but sweeter. You can try substituting steak sauce and adding a little mirin or sugar. You can find it at Japanese grocery stores.

## Pickled plums

See Umeboshi pickled plums.

## Ponzu sauce

A citrusy sauce made with citrus juice such as yuzu, lemon or lime, plus vinegar. When soy sauce is added, it's sometimes called "ponzu soy sauce." In this book, the type with soy sauce is used. Available at Japanese grocery stores or online.

## Rice vinegar

A mild-tasting vinegar brewed from rice. Do not confuse with "sushi vinegar," which often has added salt and sugar to be used as-is to make sushi rice. Rice vinegar has no additives. Available at Japanese and general Asian grocery stores and online.

## Sake

Sake is an alcoholic beverage made from rice. It's also used extensively in cooking in Japan, and is a staple in Japanese home kitchens. It is used to add flavor as well as to counteract the gamy or fishy flavors of meat and fish. Cooking sake is still sake, but has salt and sometimes other seasonings added to it.

## Sakura shrimp

Tiny dried whole shrimp that have a wonderful fragrance and are packed with flavor. The bright orange-pink color adds a nice accent to your bentos. Do not confuse with Chinese dried shrimp, which are larger; sakura shrimp are usually less than a third of an inch (8 mm) long. Available at well stocked Japanese grocery stores.

## Sesame oil

Oil made with roasted sesame seeds. It has an amber color and a rich, nutty fragrance and flavor. Available at general Asian grocery stores.

## Sesame seeds

Pre-ground sesame seeds (available at Japanese grocery stores) can be used as-is in many recipes in this book. If you can't get them pre-ground, grind up whole roasted sesame seeds roughly with a mortar and pestle or with a food mill, and store in plastic zip bags in the freezer. They can be used to absorb excess moisture in your bentos as well as to add flavor and texture.

## Seven spice

See Japanese seven spice.

## Shio kombu

Shio kombu is kombu seaweed that has been simmered until tender in a soy-sauce-based sauce. It can be used like a condiment or flavoring ingredient to add saltiness and umami. Available at Japanese grocery stores or online. If you can't find shio kombu, use crazy salt or just a pinch of ordinary salt instead.

## Shiso leaves

Shiso is a fragrant herb that is used extensively in Japanese cooking. The leaves add a nice touch of freshness to any dish. Do not confuse shiso leaves (Perilla frutescens var. Crispa) with Korean perilla or kkaennip (Perilla frutescens); although they look similar, Korean perilla has a stronger aniseed-like flavor. Green shiso is frillier and green on both sides, while Korean perilla has a purple tinge on the back side of the leaves. Fresh green shiso is available at well stocked Japanese grocery stores and some gourmet supermarkets. It's well worth growing your own too.

## Shrimp

See Sakura shrimp.

## Soy sauce

The soy sauce used in this book is regular dark (reddish brown-black) soy sauce. Use a Japanese brand if possible, since the flavor of soy sauce varies depending on which country it comes from.

## Tofu

See Abura-age tofu, Freeze-dried tofu.

## Tonkatsu sauce

This is similar to British Worcestershire sauce but with a sweeter flavor and thicker texture. You can find it at Japanese grocery stores. (The most famous brand has a bulldog on the label!)

## Udon noodles

This is another convenient noodle product that's very common in Japan. Thick wheat udon noodles are precooked and flash frozen, ready to defrost and use. You can find these frozen udon noodles at Japanese grocery stores. You can also use cooked, dried udon noodles.

## Ume paste

You can find ready-made umeboshi paste, made from the flesh of umeboshi plums, in Japanese groceries. It is sold in convenient tubes. One teaspoon of the paste equals one small umeboshi. Refrigerate after opening.

## Umeboshi pickled plums

These salt-preserved plums are related to apricots but are much tarter. They are usually quite salty and sour, although sometimes they are sweetened with sugar or honey. There are two main types: small, hard, crunchy ones, and ones with loose, soft flesh that can be chopped up. The recipes in this book use the latter type. Umeboshi keep for a long time. Store them in a cool, dark cupboard or the refrigerator. Some lower-salt versions need to be refrigerated after opening. Available at Japanese grocery stores or online.

### Wakame seaweed

Wakame seaweed is sold dried, and then reconstituted for use in soups and salads. It can also be used as-is and put under items in bentos to soak up any excess moisture! Recipes in this book use wakame that is dried and ready-cut into small pieces. Available at Japanese or general Asian grocery stores or online.

### Wasabi paste

This is the hot, green Japanese horseradish paste that is used as a condiment for sushi. A dressing called "wasabi sauce" is becoming widely available in Western supermarkets, but the recipes in this book use the paste that is sold in small tubes at Japanese groceries and increasingly in regular supermarkets.

### Yukari shiso salt

This tangy condiment is made of red shiso leaves that are dried and powdered. You can find yukari shiso salt in your Japanese grocery, or you can substitute with finely chopped umeboshi pickled plum, furikake rice sprinkles or crazy salt.

### Yuzu kosho

A condiment made with green chili paste and yuzu citrus peel. It has a citrusy fragrance and is quite spicy. Available at Japanese grocery stores or online.

## Equipment notes

- I used a 600 watt microwave oven for the recipes in this book. If the wattage of your microwave is different, please adjust the cooking times accordingly. For instance if your oven is 500 watts, increase the cooking time by 1.2 times. Be careful not to use any metal or enamel implements in a microwave.

- A fish grill, a common implement in Japanese kitchens, is used in this book. A salamander grill is very similar to a fish grill. You can use the grill in a conventional or toaster oven instead. Cooking times may vary, so check for doneness.

- Microwaved recipes are marked with an M, and grilled recipes with a G.

- A tamagoyaki pan, used in several recipes, is a square or rectangular pan that is meant for making the traditional Japanese omelet that consists of thin layers of cooked egg. You can find tamagoyaki pans online or in Japanese grocery stores. Make sure you get the right kind for the heating element on your stove. The best tamagoyaki pans are made of copper, but are quite expensive. Cheaper ones are made of aluminum and are coated with a non-stick surface. You'll find a recipe for cooking tamagoyaki in a regular frying pan on page 90.

# Bento Box Lunches Made with Real Ingredients

If you want your family to enjoy freshly made, healthy boxed lunches, but you don't always have the time to go shopping – then this book is for you. You'll find hundreds of recipes to help you make delicious and attractive bento box lunches that will get rave reviews from even the pickiest and most demanding eaters, using ingredients that you're likely to have stocked in your refrigerator.

## Great Bentos with Everyday Ingredients
# A Week of Real Bentos!

In this chapter I've recreated a week's worth of the everyday bentos I make for my kids: middle-schooler Naa, her older brother and college student Tenkichi, and occasionally their younger sister Sue. First I check what I have in the fridge, then I make everything in about ten minutes! Although I tend to use similar ingredients day to day, by varying flavors and cooking styles I'm able to create bentos that no one gets tired of, as you'll see from the comments I've included from Tenkichi, Naa and Sue.

This buttery soy chicken goes sooo well with rice!
—*My daughter Naa*

# Teriyaki Chicken Bento

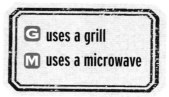

G uses a grill
M uses a microwave

## Teriyaki Chicken and Potato

**1 serving**

4 oz (100 g) chicken thigh meat
Salt, to taste
1 small potato
Vegetable oil, for cooking
1 tsp sugar
1 tsp mirin
1 tsp soy sauce
3 tsps butter

**1.** Cut the chicken into thin bite-size strips. Sprinkle with the salt and rest for 5 minutes. Peel and cut the potato into bite-size pieces, rinse briefly with water, wrap with cling film and microwave for about 90 seconds.

**2.** Put a little oil in a frying pan and put in the chicken pieces skin side down. Fry until browned. Put the microwaved potatoes in the gaps between the chicken. Add the sugar, mirin, soy sauce and butter to the pan and mix well. Turn off the heat.

## Asparagus with Miso G

**1 serving**

3 green asparagus stalks
½ tsp miso
1 tsp ground sesame seeds

**1.** Peel the asparagus stalks at the root end. Cut the stalks into 3 pieces each.

**2.** Wrap the asparagus in aluminum foil, and grill using a preheated oven or toaster oven for about 3 minutes, until the asparagus is crisp-tender. Open up the foil and coat with the miso and sesame seeds while still hot.

## Japanese Omelet

**2 servings**

2 eggs
1 Tbsp mayo
1 Tbsp water
1 tsp dried, cut wakame seaweed, optional
½ tsp soy sauce
Vegetable oil, for cooking

**1.** Mix the eggs, mayo, water, wakame seaweed and soy sauce in a bowl.

**2.** Spread some oil in a rectangular tamagoyaki pan and heat. (See page 90 for how to make Japanese omelet in a regular frying pan.) Add one third of the egg mixture and tilt the pan around to spread the mixture. When it's set, roll the egg up from the far side of the pan towards you. Repeat by adding one third each of the egg mixture, spreading it around and rolling again. Take out of the pan and cool before slicing.

19

## Salmon Spring Rolls G

**1 serving**

4 oz (100 g) fresh salmon
Salt, to taste
1 umeboshi pickled plum (or 1 tsp ume paste from a tube)
1 slice processed cheese
4 green shiso leaves
2 spring roll wrappers
2 tsps vegetable oil

1. Cut the salmon piece in half crosswise and season with salt. Leave to rest for 5 minutes. Pit the umeboshi and chop the flesh finely to turn it into a paste. Cut the cheese slice in half.

2. Place 1 piece of salmon, 2 shiso leaves, 1 piece of cheese and half the umeboshi paste on a spring roll wrapper. Roll up so the seam is on the bottom. Repeat with the other wrapper.

3. Place the spring rolls on a piece of aluminum foil and sprinkle evenly with the vegetable oil. Using a preheated oven or toaster oven grill, cook for about 6 minutes, turning the rolls over halfway through. When cooked, remove from the grill and cut each in half.

## Curried Potato and Bacon M

**1 serving**

1 medium potato
1 slice bacon, cut into small pieces
½ tsp curry powder
1 tsp sugar
1 tsp soy sauce
1 tsp butter

1. Peel the potato and cut into 1 inch (2.5 cm) dice. Rinse in cold water and drain.

2. Put the potato and bacon in a microwave-safe container and cover loosely with cling film. Microwave on the high setting for about 2½ minutes (adjust the time if needed for your microwave).

3. When a skewer goes easily through a potato piece, mix in the curry powder, sugar, soy sauce and butter while still hot.

## Stir-fried Broccoli with Almonds

**1 serving**

1 tsp sesame oil
4 cooked broccoli florets
2 tsps almond slivers
1 tsp mentsuyu sauce

1. Put the sesame oil with the broccoli and almonds in a frying pan and stir-fry. Add the mentsuyu, and continue stir-frying until the moisture in the pan has evaporated.

TUESDAY
# Salmon Spring Roll Bento
*Grilled spring rolls are pretty in pink!*

# Seafood Tempura Bento

*A hearty bento for an energy boost on hump day!*

> This seafood tempura is really crispy and delicious!
> —*My son, Tenkichi*

## Seafood Tempura

1 serving

1 cup (100 g) frozen seafood mix
1 Tbsp frozen shelled edamame beans
Salt, to taste
3 Tbsps flour
1 tsp aonori seaweed powder, or crazy salt
1 Tbsp water
Vegetable oil, for cooking
1 tsp maple syrup
1 tsp soy sauce
1 serving cooked rice

1. Defrost the seafood mix and edamame in the refrigerator overnight. Drain off excess moisture, sprinkle with the salt, flour and aonori. Toss to coat lightly, then add the water and mix quickly.

2. Heat the oil in a frying pan. Spoon in half the seafood and edamame mixture. Fry until golden on both sides. Repeat with the rest of the mixture. Drain on paper towels.

3. Mix the maple syrup and soy sauce and spoon over the hot fritters. Pack some rice into a bento box and put the fritters on top.

## Pea Shoots with Plum Ⓜ

1 serving

Handful of pea shoots
½ umeboshi pickled plum, pitted and chopped to a paste (or ½ tsp ume paste from a tube)
A few drops of vegetable stock
1 tsp ground sesame seeds

1. Cut the pea shoots in half. Wrap in cling film and microwave for 1 minute. Squeeze out the excess moisture.

2. Combine the umeboshi paste, vegetable stock, and ground sesame seeds in a bowl. Add the pea shoots and mix to coat.

## Grilled Pumpkin with Miso Ⓖ

2 servings

4 oz (100 g) deseeded kabocha or butternut squash
2 tsps butter
Pinch of salt
1 tsp maple syrup
1 tsp miso

1. Deseed the squash and slice ¼ inch (6 mm) thick. Place the slices on aluminum foil, top with the butter and sprinkle with salt. Grill using a preheated oven or toaster oven for about 7 minutes, testing for doneness. Toss with the maple syrup and miso to coat.

# Savory Pork Patty Bento

*These patties have an amazing texture!*

## Savory Pork Patties

1 serving

4 pieces thinly sliced pork, about
    4 oz (100 g)
½ carrot, slivered
1 small egg
2 tsps cornstarch
Salt and pepper, to taste
Vegetable oil, for cooking
1 Tbsp ketchup
1 tsp mirin
1 tsp soy sauce

1. Cut the pork into ½ inch (1 cm) pieces. Put
the pork, carrot, egg, cornstarch, salt and
pepper in a bowl and mix well.

2. Heat the oil in a frying pan. Divide the
pork mixture into 2 portions and spoon each
portion into the pan. Cover with a lid, and fry
on both sides till browned. Add the ketchup,
mirin and soy sauce and mix to coat.

## Spicy Spinach and Cheese

1 serving

1 slice processed cheese
¼ cup (50 g) blanched and squeezed-out
    spinach*, cut into small pieces
½ tsp gochujang bean paste
½ tsp soy sauce

1. Cut the cheese into ½ inch (1 cm) squares.

2. Put the blanched and cut up spinach, cheese,
gochujang and soy sauce in a bowl. Mix to
combine.

*For blanching instructions, see Green Leafy
Vegetables on page 11.

## Grilled Carrot and Potato G

1 serving

1 small potato, sliced into matchsticks
1 medium carrot, sliced into match-
    sticks
1 tsp sesame oil
1 Tbsp shio kombu or crazy salt

1. Rinse the potato in water and drain.

2. Put the carrot and potato on a piece of
aluminum foil and sprinkle evenly with the
sesame oil. Wrap the foil around to form a
pouch. Grill using a preheated oven or toaster
oven for about 5 minutes. Open up and foil
pouch and mix in the shio kombu.

# Teriyaki Tofu Rice-Bowl Bento

*The teriyaki flavor will make your mouth water!*

> These tofu pieces are unbelievably juicy! Sooo good!
> —*My daughter Naa*

## Teriyaki Tofu Rice Bowl

**1 serving**

1 piece freeze-dried tofu
4 thin slices pork, about 4 oz (100 g)
½ sheet nori seaweed, cut into 4
A little cornstarch
1 Tbsp sesame oil
2 Tbsps mentsuyu sauce
2 Tbsps water
1 tsp sugar
1 serving cooked rice
2 green shiso leaves
A little beni shoga red pickled ginger, or sweet pickles, for garnish
Sesame seeds, to taste

**1.** Reconstitute the tofu in water for 1 min. Slice in half horizontally, then slice in half in the middle to make 4 pieces. Wrap each piece with the pork, then the nori. Dust with the cornstarch.

**2.** Heat the oil in a frying pan. Fry the wrapped tofu, turning till brown. Add the mentsuyu, water and sugar, and toss to coat. Put the rice in a bento box and top with the shiso, tofu, pickled ginger and sesame seeds.

## Mushrooms and Green Beans with Lemon Ⓜ

**1 serving**

Handful shimeji mushrooms, or mushrooms of your choice
5 green beans
1 tsp butter
1 tsp lemon juice
A little salt

**1.** Cut the stem ends off the shimeji mushrooms, and divide into small clumps. Remove the strings and cut both ends off the green beans, and cut into thirds.

**2.** Put the mushrooms and green beans in a microwave-safe container and top with the butter. Cover loosely with cling film and microwave on the high setting for about 2 minutes. Take the cling film off while still hot, add the lemon juice and salt and mix.

## Ketchup-Potato Salad Ⓜ

**2 servings**

1 medium potato
Salt and pepper, to taste
½ tsp rice vinegar
1 Tbsp ready-made fried onions
1 tsp ketchup
1 tsp mayo

**1.** Peel the potato and cut into 1 inch (2.5 cm) dice. Rinse in cold water and drain. Put the potato pieces in a microwave-safe container and cover loosely with cling film. Microwave on the high setting for about 2 minutes until done.

**2.** Mix in the salt, pepper and vinegar while still hot, and leave to cool.

**3.** Add the fried onions, ketchup and mayo and mix to coat.

# Rice Omelet Bento

*Everyone loves this bento, particularly my daughters!*

## Rice Omelet (left)

**1 serving**
½ small green bell pepper
1 Tbsp ready-made fried onions (or use ¼ onion, chopped, instead)
1 egg
Salt and pepper, to taste
Vegetable oil
2 tsps butter
¼ cup (50 g) ground pork
2 Tbsps ketchup
1 tsp soy sauce
1 cup cooked white rice
Italian parsley, for garnish

1. Chop the bell pepper finely. (If you don't have ready-made fried onions, finely mince ¼ of an onion and sauté it before you put the bell pepper into the frying pan.) Crack the egg into a bowl, add a little salt and pepper and mix.

2. Coat a frying pan with a little vegetable oil and pour in the egg mixture. When the underside has set, flip the egg over and quickly cook the other side. Remove from the pan onto a plate.

3. Put the butter into the empty frying pan, add the ground pork and sauté. Season with salt and pepper. Add the bell pepper and sauté a little more. Add the ketchup and soy sauce and stir to evaporate some of the moisture. Add the rice, and sauté while breaking up any clumps. Add the fried onions and season again with salt and pepper, if needed.

4. Put the rice from Step 3 into a bento box and cover with the omelet from Step 2. Decorate the top with ketchup and a little Italian parsley.

## Sweet Potato with Green Beans (right) Ⓜ

**1 serving**
1 cup (150 g) sweet potato, cubed
5 green beans
Salt and pepper, to taste
1 tsp maple syrup
1 tsp lemon juice
1 tsp raisins
1 Tbsp mayo

1. Rinse the sweet potato in cold water and drain. Remove the strings and cut both ends off the green beans, and cut each one into 4 pieces.

2. Put the potato and green beans into a microwave-safe container and cover loosely with cling film. Microwave on the high setting for about 2½ minutes. Toss with the salt and pepper, maple syrup, lemon juice and raisins while still hot.

3. When the contents of the container have cooled down, mix in the mayo. Taste and adjust the seasoning if needed.

**Tip 1** The key is to flavor the other ingredients before adding the rice! If done this way the rice will not turn soggy when it's cooled.

**Tip 2** If you leave a little gap between the rice and the sides of the bento box, it's easier to cover it with the omelet.

24

This bento box is way too small for me. I need a bigger portion!
—*My daughter Naa*

25

## My Son Tenkichi's Bentos

At his high school graduation two years ago, the tearful words "Mom, thank you so much for making bentos for me every morning for three years," said by another child, not my son, made me cry. I think that was the cue for every mother there to pull out their handkerchiefs and start sniffling, although I don't even know the student that actually said it. I knew exactly how that mother must have felt to hear those words, because I too had spent the last three years making my son's bento without fail every morning—the mornings when I had a hangover; the morning I went back to sleep by mistake and only had time to make an egg fried rice bento; the mornings I forgot to switch on the rice cooker; the morning I forgot to put water in the rice cooker and ended up with a potful of piping hot raw rice; the mornings when we'd had a fight the day before, and still hadn't made up; on rainy mornings, snowy mornings, sunny mornings . . . Every morning.

He was a boy of few words, who never, ever told me "That was delicious Mom! Thank you!" or anything like that. And I know he would never say anything like "I'm sorry you have to wake up so early." And he kept on forgetting to bring home his bento box and treated the box itself so badly that it got really beaten up. I can't believe I kept on making bentos for that boy for three whole years. But now it's finally ending . . . Maybe I will never have the chance to make a bento for my oldest son again . . .

Those were my thoughts on that graduation day, as tears filled my eyes. Now, two years have passed. Tenkichi is now a sophomore in college who commutes from home. And he still takes a bento with him every day. Who would have thought? I am a happy parent, to be able to continue to make bentos for my son even now he's at college. At least, I think I am . . .

# CHAPTER 1

# The Secret to Making Delicious Bentos

The secret to making bentos that are devoured to the last morsels is to make sure the various items in the bento don't taste similar to each other. In this chapter, I'll introduce you to recipes that you can pick and choose from, organized by flavor.

My 7 Rules for Quick, Delicious Bentos

Recipes arranged by seasoning:

- Tasty and Salty-Sweet
- Simple Salt and Pepper
- Seasoned with Miso
- Seasoned with Soy Sauce
- Seasoned with Mayo
- Seasoned with Ketchup
- Seasoned with Pickled Plum
- Seasoned with Curry
- Salads & Sweet Touches

# My 7 Rules for Quick, Delicious Bentos

If you want to make bentos that will have your kids telling you "That was delicious, Mom!" just follow my rules below. These include secrets for how to speed up the bento-making process without losing any of the rave reviews!

### 1 | Season the side dishes well

The rice in a bento box is cold when it's eaten at lunchtime, so it tastes better when it's accompanied by well-seasoned sides.

### 2 | Vary the flavors

Even if you're using different ingredients, if all the items in a bento have similar flavors, they will all taste the same. There's a wide variety of recipes on pages 30 to 57 to help you make sure each item has a different flavor profile.

### 3 | Three dishes are enough

You don't need to pack lots of items for a successful bento box. As long as you make sure each item tastes different, and there's plenty of each, three dishes are more than enough.

### 4 | Separate salads and fruit from other items

Salads with savory dressings or sweet fruit and desserts shouldn't mix with other items, so it's better to put them in separate containers.

### 5 | Prep the night before

Cut up the items you'll be using for the next day's bentos while you're preparing dinner, season them with salt and pepper, cover with cling film and put them in the refrigerator ready to go. In the morning you can start cooking right away without having to pull out your cutting board, which makes things seem so much easier.

### 6 | Fully utilize your frying pan, microwave and grill

The grill in your oven can be surprisingly useful for making bentos. Just preheat the grill beforehand, wrap the ingredients in aluminum foil, and you can cook several items at once. Using the grill in parallel with your frying pan and microwave means that you can cook everything at the same time.

### 7 | Use small-serve versions of kitchen equipment

It's a waste to use large cooking implements when you're just making one or two portions. Have a few small bowls and pans on hand for quick, easy and stress-free bento making.

# Tasty and Salty-Sweet

These recipes go really well with plain rice, making them star bento players!

*Main*

## Stir-fried Beef and Egg with oyster sauce

**1 serving**

4 oz (100 g) thinly sliced beef
Vegetable oil, for cooking
1 egg, beaten with salt and pepper
1 tsp oyster sauce
Pinch of sugar
½ tsp soy sauce
Salt and pepper, to taste
A little chopped green onion (scallion)
Ground sesame seeds, to taste

1. Cut the beef into bite-size pieces. Heat the oil in a frying pan. Pour in the egg and stir to make scrambled eggs. Remove from the pan and set aside.

2. Put the beef in the empty frying pan and stir-fry until it changes color. Add the oyster sauce, sugar and soy sauce and stir. Add the onion and sesame seeds, and remove from the heat.

*Main*

*Side*

*Side*

## Honey-Mayo Chicken Ⓖ

**1 serving**

4 oz (100 g) boneless chicken thigh
1 tsp honey
1 tsp sake
2 tsps soy sauce
½ tsp cornstarch
1 to 2 Tbsps mayo
Japanese seven spice, to taste

1. Cut the chicken into bite-size pieces. Coat with the honey, sake, soy sauce and cornstarch, rub in and leave for 10 minutes.

2. Wrap the chicken in foil. Cook using a preheated grill for 8 minutes. Open the foil and spread the chicken with mayo. Grill for 1 minute. Sprinkle with Japanese seven spice.

## Soy-Simmered Bell Peppers Ⓜ

**1 serving**

2 small or 1 medium green bell pepper
1 tsp mirin
1 tsp soy sauce
Pinch of bonito flakes, optional

1. Halve and deseed the bell peppers and remove the calyxes. Slice ¾ inch (2 cm) thick. Put in a microwave-safe container and sprinkle with the mirin and soy sauce. Cover loosely with plastic wrap and microwave on the high setting for 90 seconds.

2. Add the bonito flakes and mix well.

* You can make this with zucchini or bitter melon instead.

## Butternut Squash Salad Ⓜ

**1 serving**

¾ cup (100 g) deseeded kabocha or butternut squash
A little salt
1 tsp sugar
1 tsp soy sauce
1 Tbsp mayo

1. Cut the squash into ¾ inch (2 cm) pieces. Place in a microwave-safe container, sprinkle with salt and cover loosely with cling film. Microwave on the high setting for 2½ mins. Add the sugar and soy sauce and mix.

2. When the squash has cooled completely, mash with a fork while mixing in the mayo.

* This can also be made with potato.

## Lotus Root Simmered in Sweet Vinegar

**1 serving**
4 oz (100 g) lotus root
1 Tbsp mentsuyu sauce
1 tsp rice vinegar
½ cup (125 ml) water

1. Peel the lotus root, slice into ¼ inch (6 mm) thick slices, and rinse under cold water. Drain.

2. Heat up the lotus root, mentsuyu, vinegar and water in a pan. Simmer for about 6 to 7 minutes until the lotus root is cooked through.

* Try cutting the lotus root into matchsticks instead of rounds, for a different texture.

The best! —My son, Tenkichi

## Saucy Pork and Onions

**1 serving**
3 or 4 thin slices pork, 4 oz (100 g)
Vegetable oil, for cooking
¼ medium onion, thinly sliced
1 tsp sugar
1 tsp soy sauce
1 tsp oyster sauce
1 tsp rice vinegar

1. Cut the pork into 1½ inch (4 cm) pieces.

2. Heat the oil in a frying pan. Put in the pork slices in a single layer, and fry until browned. Add the onion and stir-fry quickly. Add the sugar, soy sauce, oyster sauce and vinegar and mix to coat.

* Try making this with beef and leeks instead.

## Okonomiyaki Chicken

**1 serving**
4 oz (100 g) skinless chicken breast
Salt, pepper and sugar, to taste
1 Tbsp flour
Vegetable oil, for cooking
Okonomiyaki sauce, or steak sauce, to taste
Aonori seaweed powder, or crazy salt

1. Slice the chicken thinly. Season with the salt, pepper and sugar. Put the chicken and flour in a plastic bag, and shake to coat.

2. Heat the vegetable oil in a frying pan and put in the chicken in one layer. Fry till browned, flip and brown on the other side.

3. Spread with a little okonomiyaki sauce and sprinkle with aonori seaweed powder.

* Okonomiyaki is a savory pancake. Find okonomiyaki sauce in Japanese grocery stores.

## Pepper and Sweet Potato Stir-fry

**1 serving**
1¼ cup (200 g) sweet potato, cut into batons
1 small green bell pepper
Vegetable oil, for cooking
Pinch of shio kombu or crazy salt
1 tsp maple syrup
1 tsp soy sauce

1. Rinse the sweet potato under cold water. Drain. Deseed and slice the bell pepper thinly.

2. Heat some vegetable oil in a frying pan. Put in the sweet potato pieces in one layer, and fry until cooked through.

3. Add the bell pepper, and stir-fry until tender. Add the shio kombu, maple syrup and soy sauce and mix to combine. Remove from the heat.

They're a bit different from real croquettes. But I love them anyway!
— *My daughter Sue*

**Side**

## Tofu Croquettes Ⓜ Ⓖ

1 serving

1 medium potato, peeled
Salt and pepper, to taste
1 abura-age tofu pouch
Okonomiyaki sauce, or steak sauce, to taste
Mayo, to taste
Aonori seaweed powder, or crazy salt

1. Finely shred the potato and rinse in cold water. Put in a microwave-safe container and cover loosely with cling film. Microwave on the high setting for 90 seconds, and season with salt and pepper.

2. Cut the tofu pouch open on 3 sides and spread to form a large square. Halve to make 2 rectangles. Put half the potato on one piece and roll up. Secure with a toothpick. Repeat with the rest of the potato and tofu to make 2 rolls.

3. Wrap the rolls in foil and cook using a preheated grill for 3 minutes. Top with okonomiyaki sauce, mayo and aonori.

\* Add shredded ham or canned tuna to the potato filling.

This is really yummy!
—*My daughter Naa*

**Side**

**Side**

**Main**

## Crunchy Carrots Ⓜ

1 serving

1 medium carrot, cut into batons
Salt, to taste
1 tsp sugar
½ tsp soy sauce
½ tsp sesame oil
1 tsp ground sesame seeds

1. Place the carrots on a microwave-safe plate, sprinkle with salt and cover loosely with cling film. Microwave on the high setting for 90 seconds.

2. Sprinkle the carrots with sugar and soy sauce, and microwave, uncovered, for another minute. Sprinkle with the sesame oil and sesame seeds.

## Seafood with Potatoes

1 serving

1 medium potato
I cup (100 g) frozen seafood mix
2 tsps sake
2 tsps sugar
2 tsps soy sauce
½ cup (125 ml) water

1. Peel and cut the potato into ¾ inch (2 cm) pieces. Rinse under cold water and drain. Put the seafood mix in a colander and rinse under cold water to remove the surface ice.

2. Put the other ingredients in a pan and bring to a boil. Add the seafood mix, and simmer for 7–8 minutes, till no moisture is left in the pan.

\* You can make this with frozen peeled shrimp or cut up squid instead.

## Sweet & Sour Crispy Pork

1 serving

4 thin slices pork, 4 oz (100 g)
Salt and pepper, to taste
Cornstarch, for dusting
Vegetable oil, for cooking
1 Tbsp mentsuyu sauce
1 tsp rice vinegar
½ tsp sugar

1. Cut the pork into bite-size pieces. Season with the salt and pepper and dust on both sides with cornstarch.

2. Heat the oil in a frying pan. Put in the pork in one layer and fry on both sides. Push the pork to one side, pour out excess oil and add the mentsuyu, vinegar and sugar. Bring to a boil and mix with the pork to coat it.

Let them know that Naa highly recommends this!
—My daughter Naa

(Main)

(Side)

(Main)

## Sweet & Spicy Mackerel

1 serving

1 boneless mackerel fillet
Salt and pepper, to taste
A little sake
Cornstarch, for dusting
Vegetable oil, for cooking
1 tsp gochujang bean paste
1 tsp sugar
1 tsp soy sauce

1. Cut the mackerel into bite-size pieces. Sprinkle with the salt, pepper and sake, and rest for about 10 minutes. Pat the fish dry, and dust with cornstarch.

2. Shallow fry the fish in one layer, turning until crispy. Mix gochujang, sugar and soy sauce in a bowl. Put the fish into this sauce, and leave to soak for a few minutes.

## Soy-Simmered Cabbage

1 serving (M)

2 cabbage leaves
1 Tbsp sakura shrimp
1 tsp mirin
1 tsp soy sauce

1. Cut the cabbage into bite-size pieces. Put into a microwave-safe container.

2. Add the sakura shrimp, mirin and soy sauce to the container and cover loosely with cling film. Microwave on the high setting for about 2 minutes.

* Add a little Japanese seven spice for an extra kick!

## Mushroom and Pork Rolls

1 serving

1 king oyster mushroom
4 pieces thinly sliced pork, about 4 oz (100 g)
Salt and pepper, to taste
Vegetable oil, for cooking
1 tsp tonkatsu sauce
1 tsp sugar
½ tsp soy sauce

1. Slice the king oyster mushroom in half lengthwise, then cut into matchsticks.

2. Spread out the pork slices, place the cut mushrooms on top and roll up the pork. Season with salt and pepper.

3. Heat the oil in a frying pan. Put the rolls in the pan, seam sides facing down. Fry while turning until browned. Lower the heat and add the tonkatsu sauce, sugar and soy sauce. Turn the rolls to coat in the sauce.

## Spicy Chicken with Green Beans

1 serving

4 oz (100 g) boneless chicken thigh
Pinch of salt
1 tsp honey
2 tsps soy sauce
¼ tsp doubanjiang chili bean paste
4 green beans, trimmed
Vegetable oil, for cooking

1. Cut the chicken into bite-size pieces. Marinate in the salt, honey, soy sauce and doubanjiang for 10 minutes. Cut the green beans into 1½ inch (4 cm) pieces.

2. Heat the oil in a frying pan. Put in the chicken, skin side down in a single layer. Sauté slowly over low heat, making sure not to let it burn. Add the green beans, cover with a lid and steam cook until done. Turn off the heat. Shake the pan to reduce the sauce.

* You can use green asparagus or sugar snap peas instead of the green beans.

(Main)

# Simple Salt and Pepper

Everything tastes great simply seasoned this way, and you don't get bored with it!

*Main*

*I like this with lots and lots of peppers!*
*—My daughter Naa*

## Chicken & Pepper Stir-fry

**1 serving**
4 oz (100 g) skinless chicken breast
2 small or 1 medium green bell pepper
Salt and pepper, to taste
A little sake
Cornstarch, for dusting
Sesame oil, for cooking
A few drops of chicken stock, to taste

1. Thinly slice the chicken and bell peppers. Season the chicken with salt, pepper, and sake, dust with cornstarch and rub it in well.

2. Heat up some sesame oil in a frying pan, and stir-fry the chicken. When it changes color add the bell pepper and continue stir-frying. Add the stock and mix.

## Grilled Sweet Potato G

**1 serving**
4 slices sweet potato, in ½ inch
(1 cm) rounds
Pinch of salt
1 tsp sesame oil*

1. Rinse the sweet potato slices in cold water and drain. Put the slices on a piece of foil.

2. Sprinkle the potato with salt and sesame oil. Preheat the grill, wrap the potato in the foil and grill for 7 minutes. Turn off the heat and leave to cook in residual heat for 5 minutes.

* You can use olive oil instead of sesame oil. This sweet bento item is nice change of pace.

## Salt & Sesame Cabbage

**1 serving** M
1 to 2 cabbage leaves
Pinch of salt
1 tsp sesame oil
1 tsp ground sesame seeds

1. Cut the cabbage into bite-size pieces and place in a microwave-safe container. Cover the container loosely with cling film and microwave on the high setting for 1 min.

2. Add the salt, sesame oil and seeds. Mix.

* This lightly flavored side dish goes well with strongly flavored main dishes.

## Herb-Grilled Lotus Root

**1 serving** G
4 oz (100 g) lotus root, peeled
1 tsp olive oil
Salt and mixed dried herbs, to taste

1. Cut the lotus root into quarters lengthwise. Cut into ½ inch (1 cm) slices, rinse in water and drain. Sprinkle with the olive oil and place on a sheet of foil. Wrap the foil around the lotus root and grill for about 7 minutes.

2. When the lotus root is firm yet tender and a skewer goes easily through a slice, sprinkle with the salt and herb mix and toss to coat.

* Try using bell peppers, zucchini, green beans or nagaimo yam instead of lotus root.

# Crunchy Chicken Patties

**1 serving**

**2 oz (50 g) lotus root, peeled**
**¼ cup (50 g) ground chicken**
**½ beaten egg**
**1 tsp cornstarch**
**Salt and pepper, to taste**
**Green part of a green onion (scallion), finely chopped**
**Sesame oil, for cooking**

1. Dice the lotus root, rinse in cold water and drain. Mix all ingredients, except the oil, in a bowl.

2. Heat the sesame oil in a frying pan, and drop in spoonfuls of the chicken mixture. Brown on one side, flip over and cover the pan with a lid until both sides are browned and cooked through.

# Celery with Sesame Ⓜ

**1 serving**

**½ stalk celery**
**Pinch of shio kombu or crazy salt**
**1 tsp sesame oil**
**1 tsp ground sesame seeds**

1. Chop the celery up roughly and put into a microwave-safe container. Cover loosely with cling film and microwave on the high setting for about 1 minute.

2. Add the shio kombu, sesame oil and sesame seeds and mix.

* Try this with bell pepper instead of celery.

# Simple Sautéed Chicken

**1 serving**

**4 oz (100 g) boneless chicken breast**
**Salt and pepper, to taste**
**1 Tbsp flour**
**Vegetable oil, for cooking**
**A few drops of chicken stock, to taste**

1. Slice the chicken diagonally into thin slices. Season with salt and pepper.

2. Put the chicken and flour into a plastic bag and shake to coat the chicken evenly.

3. Heat up the vegetable oil in a frying pan, and put in the chicken. Brown on both sides. Add the chicken stock while the chicken is still hot and toss to coat.

* Try adding some grainy mustard, ume paste or wasabi to the chicken stock. Delicious!

# Sesame Pork with Pea Shoots

**1 serving**

**2 to 3 pieces thinly sliced pork, about 3 oz (75 g)**
**Small handful of pea shoots**
**Sesame oil, for stir-frying**
**A few drops of stock, to taste**
**1 tsp ground sesame seeds**

1. Cut the pork and the pea shoots into 1 inch (2.5 cm) pieces.

2. Heat up some sesame oil in a frying pan and stir-fry the pork. Wipe out the excess fat from the frying pan and add the pea shoots. Add the stock and simmer until the pea shoots are tender. Turn off the heat and sprinkle in the sesame seeds.

* Try using mitsuba leaves or celery instead of the pea shoots.

*I love this one!*
*—My daughter Sue*

I love salted salmon so much!
—*My daughter Naa*

## Salted Salmon G

1 serving

**1 fresh salmon fillet, about 4 oz (100 g)**
**Salt**
**Green onion (scallion), for garnish, optional**

1. Sprinkle the salmon evenly and generously on both sides with salt. Wrap tightly in cling film and refrigerate overnight.

2. The next day, unwrap the salmon and pat dry with paper towels. Wrap the salmon in aluminum foil and place under a preheated oven grill. Cook for about 7 minutes. Top with green onion if you like.

* You can use cod or mackerel instead of salmon. You can serve the salmon on a bed of rice with shredded nori seaweed for a hearty "rice-bowl" type bento.

This was good.
—*Naa, who calls broccoli "forest."*

## Sesame Bell Peppers M

1 serving

**2 small or 1 medium bell pepper (here I've used a mix of green and orange peppers)**
**1 tsp sesame oil**
**A pinch of shio kombu or crazy salt**

1. Slice the bell pepper into thin rounds, removing the seeds as you cut. Put the slices in a microwave-safe container, mix in the sesame oil and shio kombu, and cover the container loosely with cling film.

2. Microwave on the high setting for about 90 seconds.

* You can add a little mirin too for a touch of sweetness. If the bell pepper becomes too watery, add some ground sesame seeds, which will absorb the excess moisture.

## Japanese-Style Broccoli M

1 serving

**4 broccoli florets**
**A few drops of vegetable stock**

1. Cut the broccoli into bite size pieces, place in a microwave-safe container and cover loosely with cling film. Microwave on the high setting for about a minute.

2. Sprinkle with the vegetable stock while still hot.

* This is also great made with spinach, cabbage or bok choy instead of broccoli.

## Grilled Onions G

1 serving

**½ medium onion**
**1 tsp dried parsley**
**2 tsps olive oil**
**A pinch of salt**

1. Cut the onion into wedges.

2. Spread out a piece of aluminum foil and put the onion and parsley on it. Sprinkle with olive oil and salt. Wrap the foil around the onion.

3. Place the foil packet under a preheated oven grill for about 5 minutes.

# Spicy Potato and Carrot M

**1 serving**

**1 small potato**
**1 medium carrot**
**A few drops of vegetable stock**
**1 tsp sesame oil**
**1 tsp ground sesame seeds**
**Karashi mustard or English mustard,**
**    to taste, optional**

1. Peel the potato and cut into matchsticks. Rinse in cold water and drain. Peel and cut the carrot into matchsticks too.

2. Put the potato and carrot in a microwave-safe container and cover loosely with cling film. Microwave on the high setting for about 2½ minutes. Mix with the other ingredients while still hot.

# Steamed Eggplant M

**1 serving**

**2 oz (50 g) eggplant, roughly chopped**
**Salt, to taste**
**1 tsp sesame oil**
**¼ green onion (scallion)**

1. Put the eggplant pieces into a microwave-safe container. Sprinkle with salt and sesame oil and cover loosely with cling film. Microwave on the high setting for about 2 minutes. Finely chop the green onion.

2. Remove the cling film and add the green onion to the eggplant. Mix everything together.

* This is delicious with a little wasabi or yuzu kosho (a spicy condiment made with yuzu citrus and green chili peppers) too.

# Tofu Fritters

**1 serving**

**1 sheet freeze-dried tofu**
**A few drops of vegetable stock**
**1 Tbsp water**
**Black pepper, to taste**
**Cornstarch, for dusting**
**Vegetable oil**

1. Soak the tofu in a bowl of water for a minute. Squeeze to remove the water. Cut into 6 pieces, put in a bowl with the stock powder and water, and squeeze with your hands so that the liquid is absorbed.

2. Sprinkle with the pepper, then dust with cornstarch. Heat a generous amount of oil in a frying pan. Add the tofu pieces so they don't touch each other. Shallow fry on both sides until golden brown and crispy, take out of the oil and drain.

# Mini Pork Patties

**1 serving**

**4 pieces thinly sliced pork, about**
**    4 oz (100 g)**
**3 green shiso leaves**
**Salt and pepper, to taste**
**1 Tbsp mayo**
**1 Tbsp cornstarch**
**Vegetable oil, for frying**

1. Dice the pork slices and shiso leaves. Place in a bowl with a generous amount of salt and pepper, the mayo and the cornstarch and mix together well.

2. Heat up some oil in a frying pan. Divide the meat mixture into 4 portions, form each into a small patty (about 1 Tbsp each) and pan-fry on both sides until golden brown.

* To form neat patties, try using a soup spoon.

Mom, can you make these again?
—Sue

# Seasoned with Miso

Rich, salty miso really enhances the flavor of ingredients, and miso dishes go great with rice. Find out more about this Japanese kitchen staple on page 13.

*(Main)*

> I just looove eggplant!
> —My daughter Naa

## Pork and Eggplant Rolls

1 serving
2 oz (50 g) eggplant
4 pieces thinly sliced pork, total weight about 4 oz (100 g)
Sesame oil, for cooking
1 Tbsp mentsuyu sauce
1 tsp miso
Sesame seeds, to taste

1. Cut the eggplant into 2 inch (5 cm) lengths. Soak in a bowl of salted water for a minute. Drain very well. Place ¼ of the eggplant on a piece of pork, and roll it up. Repeat with the rest of the pork and eggplant.

2. Heat the oil in a frying pan. Put in the pork rolls seam side down. Cover with a lid and steam-fry, turning occasionally, until cooked through. Add the mentsuyu and miso. Toss to coat. Sprinkle with sesame seeds.

* Use pork belly for a rich taste, and pork loin for a lighter version.

*(Main)*

*(Side)*

*(Side)*

## Chicken in Miso Sauce Ⓜ

1 serving
4 oz (100 g) skinless chicken thigh
1 heaping tsp miso
1 heaping tsp honey
¾ tsp grated ginger
Chopped green onion (scallion), for garnish

1. Slice the chicken thinly diagonally. Mix with the miso, honey and ginger, and marinate for 15 minutes. Wrap each piece of chicken in kitchen parchment paper, twisting each end closed. Put on a microwave-safe plate, and microwave on the high setting for 2 minutes. Turn, unwrap and microwave for another minute. Garnish with the green onion.

## Spinach with Sesame-Miso Ⓜ

1 serving
1 tsp miso
½ tsp maple syrup
¼ bunch spinach*, blanched and squeezed out**
1 tsp ground sesame seeds

1. Combine the miso and maple syrup in a small microwave-safe container. Microwave on the high setting for 10 seconds to soften.

2. Mix the miso-maple syrup sauce with the spinach. Add sesame seeds and mix again.

* Try with bok choy or komatsuna instead.
** See blanching instructions on page 11.

## Miso Potatoes Ⓜ

1 serving
1 potato, peeled
1 tsp sugar
1 tsp miso
1 tsp mentsuyu sauce
1 tsp black sesame seeds

1. Cut the potato into 1 inch (2.5 cm) pieces. Rinse in water and drain. Put in a microwave-safe container, cover loosely with cling film and microwave on the high setting for 2 mins.

2. Drain off any excess water while the potatoes are still hot. Return to the container and add the sugar, miso and mentsuyu. Microwave, uncovered, for another 20 seconds. Leave until cool, and sprinkle with the black sesame seeds.

## Chicken with Sweet Miso

**1 serving**
4 oz (100 g) skinless chicken breast
Salt and pepper, to taste
1 Tbsp flour
2 tsps miso
2 tsps honey
A little butter
Vegetable oil, for cooking

1. Slice the chicken thinly diagonally. Season with salt and pepper.

2. Put the chicken and flour in a plastic bag, and shake to coat the chicken. Combine the miso, honey and butter in a small bowl.

3. Heat up some vegetable oil in a frying pan. Add the chicken in a single layer and pan-fry until golden brown on both sides. Take out the chicken when cooked and put into the bowl with the miso, honey and butter. Mix well to coat while the chicken is still hot.

## Cabbage with Mustard-Miso Mayo

**1 serving**
2 cabbage leaves
1 tsp mayo
½ tsp karashi mustard or English mustard
½ tsp miso

1. Cut the cabbage up into bite-size pieces.

2. Heat the mayo in a frying pan and stir-fry the cabbage. When the cabbage is tender, turn down the heat and add the mustard and miso. Mix well.

* Brown the cabbage a little to give it a nutty flavor.

## Cheese and Tofu Rolls Ⓖ

**1 serving**
½ abura-age tofu pouch
1 Tbsp cream cheese
1 green shiso leaf
½ tsp miso

1. Halve the tofu pouch, cream cheese and shiso leaf. Spread the tofu on one side with the miso. Place a piece of shiso leaf and a portion of cream cheese on each tofu piece, roll up and secure with toothpicks.

2. Preheat the grill. Wrap the rolls in foil (so the toothpicks don't burn). Grill for about 5 minutes.

* You can use sliced cheese instead of the cream cheese. Try adding umeboshi pickled plum paste.

## Lotus Root and Chicken with Miso

**1 serving**
4 oz (100 g) skinless chicken thigh
Salt, to taste,
A little sake
2 oz (50 g) lotus root
Green part of a green onion (scallion)
Vegetable oil, for cooking
1 Tbsp miso

1. Cut the chicken into bite-size pieces. Sprinkle with salt and sake, and rub them in with your hands. Peel and roughly chop the lotus root and rinse in water; drain. Finely chop the green onion.

2. Heat up some vegetable oil in a frying pan. Put the chicken in in a single layer, and pan-fry until it changes color. Turn and cook on the other side. Put the lotus root in the empty spaces in the frying pan and stir-fry.

3. Add the miso and mix well. Turn off the heat and continue cooking with the residual heat. Garnish with the green onion.

*So good with rice!*
*—My daughter Naa*

## Chicken with Miso Mayo

1 serving

**2 chicken tenders, about 4 oz (100 g)**
**Salt and pepper, to taste**
**Cornstarch**
**Vegetable oil, for cooking**
**1 Tbsp mayo**
**½ Tbsp miso**
**Chopped parsley, for garnish**

1. Remove the sinew from the chicken tenders. Diagonally slice each tender in half. Season with salt and pepper, and dust with cornstarch.

2. Heat up some vegetable oil in a frying pan. Pan-fry the chicken in the oil while turning.

3. Mix the mayo and miso together in a small bowl. Put in the cooked hot chicken and mix well. Sprinkle with some chopped parsley.

* Add a little doubanjiang to make this spicy.

Main

Side

Side

## Pork & Peppers with Miso

1 serving

**2 small or 1 medium bell pepper**
**4 pieces thinly sliced pork, about 4 oz (100 g), cut in thin strips**
**Salt and pepper, to taste**
**1 tsp cornstarch**
**Sesame oil, for cooking**
**1 tsp miso**
**1 tsp soy sauce**
**1 tsp sugar**

1. Cut the pepper into thin strips. Rub the pork with salt, pepper and cornstarch.

2. Heat the sesame oil in a frying pan. Stir-fry the pork. When it changes color add the bell pepper and continue stir-frying. Add the miso, soy sauce and sugar and mix to coat.

## Carrot with Miso Sauce

1 serving   Ⓜ

**1 small carrot**
**½ tsp rice vinegar**
**2 tsp miso**

1. Cut the carrot into batons, wrap with cling film and microwave on the high setting for about a minute.

2. Add the vinegar and miso to the carrot and mix while still hot. Leave to cool.

* Don't overcook the carrots. They should just be crisp-tender.

## Pumpkin with Miso Butter

1 serving   Ⓜ

**¾ cup (100 g) deseeded kabocha or butternut squash**
**1 tsp honey**
**1 tsp miso**
**1 teaspoon butter**

1. Cut the squash into bite-size pieces. Place in a microwave-safe container skin side down, and cover loosely with cling film. Microwave on the high setting for about 2½ minutes.

2. Add the honey, miso and butter while the squash is still hot and mix to coat. Microwave for an additional 20 seconds.

* You can make this with sweet potato too.

## Grilled Onion with Miso Mayo G

**1 serving**
**¼ onion**
**1 tsp miso**
**Mayo, to taste**

1. Cut the onion into ½ inch (1 cm) slices. Secure the slices with toothpicks so the layers don't fall apart. Preheat the grill. Wrap the onion in aluminum foil and grill for about 6 minutes.

2. When the onion slices are tender, spread with miso and mayo. Wrap the toothpicks with foil so they don't get burned (the onion slices don't have to be covered) and grill for another minute.

\* Miso burns easily so watch these carefully! Try sprinkling on some Japanese seven spice.

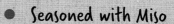

## Eggplant with Plum Miso M

**1 serving**
**2 oz (50 g) eggplant**
**1 tsp miso**
**½ umeboshi pickled plum (or ½ tsp ume paste)**

1. Cut the eggplant up roughly and place in a microwave-safe container. Cover loosely with cling film and microwave on the high setting for about 2 minutes.

2. Add the miso and pitted and chopped umeboshi (or ume paste) to the cooked eggplant and mix.

\* Make this taste richer by adding a little sesame oil.

## Broccoli and Pasta Miso Salad

**1 serving**
**Handful quick-cook short pasta such as macaroni or penne**
**4 broccoli florets**
**1 tsp miso**
**1 Tbsp cream cheese**
**Salt and pepper, to taste**

1. Bring a pan of salted water to a boil. Add the pasta, then the broccoli and cook until the pasta is done. Drain into a colander.

2. Return the pasta and broccoli to the pan while still hot, add the miso, cream cheese and salt and pepper and mix well.

\* You can add mayo instead of the cream cheese. Try green beans or sugar snap peas instead of the broccoli.

## Creamy Miso Potatoes M

**1 serving**
**4 green beans**
**1 small potato**
**1 Tbsp cream cheese**
**1 tsp miso**
**½ tsp maple syrup**

1. Remove the strings and cut both ends off the green beans and cut in half. Peel and cut the potato into matchsticks and rinse in water; drain.

2. Put the green beans and potato in a microwave-safe container and cover loosely with cling film. Microwave on the high setting for about 2 minutes. Add the cream cheese, miso and maple syrup while still hot and mix well.

\* This is also delicious with a little ume paste added to the sauce.

# Seasoned with Soy Sauce

Soy sauce can be combined with mustard, bonito flakes and other flavorings for endless variety!

*(Main)*

> Celery is delicious. I can't understand why some people don't like it!
> —*My daughter Naa*

## Pork and Celery Noodles

2 servings

Sesame oil, for cooking
3 to 4 pieces thinly sliced pork, about 4 oz (100 g), cut in bite-size pieces
½ stalk celery, thinly sliced
Salt and pepper, to taste
½ cup (125 ml) water
2 oz (50 g) uncooked glass noodles
1 Tbsp soy sauce

1. Heat the oil in a frying pan. Add the pork and stir-fry until it changes color. Add the celery and continue stir-frying.

2. Add the salt and pepper, and the water. Add the glass noodles and stir as they reconstitute. Add the soy sauce, stir till most of the moisture in the pan has evaporated.

* Use short, precut glass noodles that don't need to be presoaked, if possible. If not, soak the noodles in hot water until softened, drain well and cut up before putting in the pan.

*(Main)*

## Pork with Mustard-Soy Sauce

1 serving

4 pieces thinly sliced pork, about 4 oz (100 g)
1 green onion (scallion), finely chopped
⅓ tsp karashi mustard or English mustard
1½ tsps soy sauce

1. Cut the pork into bite-size pieces. Bring some water to a boil in a pan and boil the pork in it briefly. Rinse under cold water, drain well and pat dry with paper towels. Put all ingredients in a bowl and mix well.

* Boiled and rinsed pork has less surface fat, fewer calories, and no fatty residue on the pork when it's cooled, which is a plus.

*(Main)*

## Salmon and Green Beans in Soy Sauce Ⓖ

1 serving

4 oz (100 g) fresh salmon fillet
Salt, for sprinkling
1 tsp soy sauce
3 green beans, trimmed and halved
1 tsp yuzu kosho, optional

1. Sprinkle the salmon fillet with salt and wrap it in cling film. Refrigerate overnight.

2. Put the unwrapped salmon and green beans on a piece of foil, and wrap up to make a packet. Grill for 7 minutes. Sprinkle with the soy sauce and yuzu kosho while still hot. Leave to cool.

*(Side)*

## Fish Sticks with Cheese

1 serving

2 chikuwa fish sticks*
5 green beans, trimmed
Vegetable oil, for cooking
1 tsp soy sauce
2 tsps grated cheese

1. Cut the chikuwa into bite-size diagonal pieces. Slice the green beans.

2. Heat the oil in a frying pan. Add the chikuwa and green beans, and stir-fry until the green beans are limp and lightly browned. Sprinkle with the soy sauce and cheese.

*You can use frankfurters instead of chikuwa.

## Cheese & Cabbage Rolls

**Side**

**G M**

**1 serving**

1 abura-age tofu pouch
1–2 cabbage leaves
1 slice processed cheese, halved
Soy sauce, to taste

1. Cut the tofu pouch on 3 sides and open it up so that you have one big square piece. Cut in half to make 2 rectangular pieces. Put the cabbage leaves in a microwave-safe container and cover loosely with cling film. Microwave on the high setting for a minute, shred and squeeze out excess moisture.

2. Place the half slice of cheese and half the cabbage on each piece of tofu, and roll up tightly. Secure with toothpicks.

3. Wrap the rolls in foil. Grill for 3 minutes. Open up the foil and sprinkle with soy sauce. Cut the rolls into bite-size pieces.

## Savory Cabbage **M**

**Side**

**1 serving**

1 cabbage leaf
1 Tbsp dried, cut wakame seaweed, optional
Pinch of salt
1 tsp soy sauce
Pinch of bonito flakes, optional

1. Cut the cabbage into bite-size pieces. Put the wakame seaweed in a bowl of water for a minute or so, and drain.

2. Put the cabbage and wakame seaweed in a microwave-safe container. Sprinkle with salt and cover loosely with cling film. Microwave on the high setting for about 90 seconds.

3. Sprinkle with soy sauce while still hot. Add the bonito flakes at the end.

## Mustard-Soy Chicken

**Main**

**1 serving**

4 oz (100 g) boneless chicken breast
Salt, pepper and sugar, to taste
1 Tbsp flour
Vegetable oil, for cooking
1 tsp soy sauce
1 tsp karashi mustard or English mustard
1 Tbsp chopped green onion (scallion)

1. Slice the chicken into thin diagonal pieces. Season with salt, pepper and a little sugar. Put the chicken in a plastic bag with the flour. Shake to coat evenly.

2. Heat the oil in a frying pan, and put in the chicken in a single layer. Brown on both sides. When cooked, put the chicken in the bowl with the soy sauce and mustard, and mix to coat. Top with the green onion.

## Tofu Steaks with Soy Sauce

**2 servings**

2 pieces freeze-dried tofu
1 egg
Handful bonito flakes, optional
Pinch of salt
Vegetable oil, for cooking
2 tsps butter
1 tsp soy sauce

1. Soak the freeze-dried tofu in water for about 1 minute to reconstitute. Squeeze out the excess water and slice in half horizontally, so you end up with 4 thin pieces.

2. Put the egg, bonito flakes and salt in a bowl and mix well. Put in the freeze-dried tofu and let the egg mixture permeate it.

3. Heat up some vegetable oil and the butter in a frying pan. Add the freeze-dried tofu and brown on both sides.

4. Add the soy sauce to the hot side of the pan, and mix to coat.

\* Add some shredded nori seaweed for even more flavor.

**Main**

*I love tofu, especially on rice! —My daughter Sue*

43

## Speedy Noodle Stir-Fry

1 serving

2 chikuwa fish sticks*
1 cabbage leaf
1 tsp sesame oil
1 serving cooked Chinese noodles
1 Tbsp chopped pickled mustard
    greens (takanazuke, from your
    Japanese grocery store)
2 tsps soy sauce

1. Slice the chikuwa lengthwise. Cut the cabbage into bite-size pieces.

2. Heat the oil in a frying pan and stir-fry the noodles. Add the chikuwa and cabbage and continue stir-frying. When the cabbage is tender, add the chopped pickled mustard greens and soy sauce, and mix well.

* Try thinly sliced meat or mixed frozen seafood instead of the chikuwa. Try pre-cooked pasta, instant ramen noodles or rice instead of Chinese noodles.

## Spinach & Ginger Tofu

G

1 serving

¼ abura-age tofu pouch
¼ cup (50 g) blanched and squeezed-
    out spinach (see page 11)
½ tsp grated ginger
1 tsp soy sauce

1. Put a sheet of foil under a preheated grill. Grill the tofu for 5 minutes until crisp.

2. Let the tofu cool, and cut into bite-size pieces. Cut up the spinach, and put in a bowl with the tofu, ginger and soy sauce and mix.

* You can use komatsuna greens or other dark greens instead of spinach.

## Spicy Eggplant

1 serving

2 oz (50 g) eggplant
A little salt
1 tsp soy sauce
1 tsp karashi mustard or English
    mustard

1. Cut the eggplant into batons. Fill a bowl with water and add the salt. Put the eggplant in the salt water for a minute. Drain.

2. Mix the eggplant in a bowl with the soy sauce and mustard. The flavors will penetrate the eggplant in 10 minutes, but you can make this the night before too.

## Pumpkin with Soy Sauce

M

2 servings

¾ cup (100 g) deseeded kabocha or
    butternut squash
Salt, to taste
1 tsp butter
1 tsp soy sauce
Handful bonito flakes, optional

1. Cut the squash into 1 inch (2.5 cm) pieces. Put into a microwave-safe container, skin side down. Sprinkle with salt, top with the butter, and cover loosely with cling film. Microwave on the high setting for 2½ minutes.

2. Remove the cling film, drizzle on the soy sauce and mix. Sprinkle with the bonito flakes.

* Try with sweet potato or taro root instead.

## Pork & Eggplant Soboro

**1 serving**
**2 oz (50 g) eggplant, diced**
**1 tsp sesame oil**
**¼ cup (50 g) ground pork**
**Salt and pepper, to taste**
**1 tsp grated garlic**
**2 tsps soy sauce**

1. Put the eggplant in a bowl of salted water for a minute. Drain well.

2. Heat the oil in a frying pan and stir-fry the pork. When it changes color add the eggplant and continue stir-frying. Add the other ingredients and keep stir-frying until very little moisture is left in the pan.

* (See page 77 for more on soboro dishes).

## Seafood in Soy Sauce

**1 serving**
**½ cup (50 g) frozen seafood mix**
**Handful shimeji mushrooms, or mushrooms of your choice**
**1 Tbsp sake**
**½ Tbsp soy sauce**
**2 tsps butter**

1. Rinse the seafood briefly under running water to remove the surface ice, and drain. Trim the mushrooms and break into clumps.

2. Put the seafood, mushrooms, sake and soy sauce in a small pan. Cook on medium heat until the mushrooms are limp. Add the butter and cook until there is little moisture left in the pan.

## Savory Carrot Pancakes

**1 serving**
**1 large carrot, finely shredded**
**Pinch of salt**
**1 tsp ground sesame seeds**
**3 Tbsps flour**
**2 Tbsps water**
**1 tsp sesame oil**
**1 tsp soy sauce**

1. Sprinkle the carrot with the salt, and rub in until the carrot turns limp. Squeeze out tightly to remove excess moisture.

2. Put the carrot, sesame seeds and flour in a bowl and mix well. Add the water and mix.

3. Heat the oil in a frying pan. Put in the carrot mixture and press it flat. Fry, turning, until browned on both sides. Cut into easy-to-eat pieces, and sprinkle with soy sauce.

* This is a simple version of Korean pancakes or buchimgae. You can make this with garlic chives or pea shoots too.

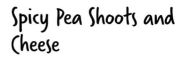

## Spicy Pea Shoots and Cheese

**1 serving**
**Handful of pea shoots**
**1 slice processed cheese**
**½ tsp wasabi paste**
**1 tsp soy sauce**
**1 tsp ground sesame seeds**

1. Cut the pea shoots into 1 inch (2.5 cm) lengths. Bring a pot of water to a boil, add the pea shoots and boil for a minute. Drain and cool under cold running water. Drain and squeeze out tightly. Dice the cheese.

2. Combine the blanched pea shoots, cheese, wasabi, soy sauce and sesame seeds and mix well.

* You can microwave the pea shoots instead of blanching them.

# Seasoned with Mayo

Cooking hot dishes with mayo adds richness as well as slight acidity. Give it a try!

**Main**

## Mackerel with Mayo

1 serving
1 piece mackerel
1 Tbsp sake
Salt and pepper, to taste
1 tsp mayo
1 tsp soy sauce
Cornstarch, for dusting
Vegetable oil, for cooking

1. Cut the mackerel into bite-size pieces. Sprinkle with the sake, salt and pepper and leave for about 10 minutes.

2. Pat the fish dry with paper towel. Combine the mayo and soy sauce and coat the fish pieces with it, then dust with the cornstarch.

3. Heat up a generous amount of oil in a frying pan. Shallow fry the fish pieces while turning them frequently, until golden brown.

*You can use salmon for this recipe too.

**Main**

## Mayo Pork & Mushrooms

1 serving
Handful shimeji mushrooms, or mush-
    rooms of your choice
1 Tbsp mayo
3 to 4 pieces thinly sliced pork, about
    4 oz (100 g)
Salt and pepper, to taste
1 tsp soy sauce

1. Cut the stem ends off the shimeji and divide into small clumps. Heat the mayo in a frying pan. Add the pork, and stir-fry, coating with the mayo. When the meat changes color, add the shimeji and stir-fry until limp. Season with the salt, pepper and soy sauce and mix well.

**Side**

## Spicy Mayo Cabbage Ⓖ

1 serving
2 cabbage leaves
Salt, to taste
1 Tbsp mayo
1 small red chili pepper, sliced in thin
    rounds, or ground chili pepper

1. Cut the cabbage into bite-size pieces.

2. Place the cabbage on a piece of foil, sprinkle with salt and wrap the foil around.

3. Cook the foil packet under a preheated grill for 4 minutes. Open the packet and add the mayo and chili pepper. Mix well to coat.

**Side**

## Tangy Carrot Salad Ⓜ

1 serving
1 small carrot
1 chikuwa fish stick, or frankfurter
1 tsp sesame oil
1 tsp mayo
1 tsp yukari shiso salt or finely
    chopped umeboshi pickled plum

1. Shred the carrot. Cut the chikuwa fish stick into matchsticks.

2. Put the carrot and chikuwa in a microwave-safe container and drizzle on the sesame oil. Cover loosely with cling film and microwave on the high setting for 1 minute.

3. Mix well with the mayo and yukari.

## Mini Omelets

1 serving

¼ cup (50 g) ground chicken or any other ground meat

Green part of a green onion (scallion), finely chopped

1 egg

1 Tbsp cornstarch

1 Tbsp mayo

Pinch of shio kombu or crazy salt

Vegetable oil, for cooking

1. Put all ingredients in a bowl and mix well.

2. Heat the oil in a frying pan, and drop spoonfuls of the mixture into the pan. Cook on both sides until golden brown, turning occasionally.

* Ground pork, beef or any ground meat of your choice can be used.

*These are the best!
—My daughter Sue*

## Broccoli with Sesame Mayo

1 serving

4 cooked broccoli florets

Pinch of salt

2 tsps mayo

½ tsp sugar

½ tsp soy sauce

½ tsp rice vinegar

1 tsp ground sesame seeds

1. Mix the broccoli with the other ingredients.

* This can be made with blanched spinach too.

## Oyster Sauce Chicken

1 serving

½ skinless chicken breast

Salt and pepper, to taste

1 Tbsp flour

1 tsp mayo

1 tsp oyster sauce

Vegetable oil, for cooking

1. Cut the chicken into thin diagonal slices. Season with salt and pepper. Put the chicken and flour in a plastic bag. Shake to coat the chicken with the flour. Mix the mayo and oyster sauce on a small plate.

2. Heat the oil in a frying pan. Put in the chicken in one layer, and brown on both sides. Put the cooked chicken on the plate from Step 1 while still hot, and turn several times to coat with the sauce.

## Noodles with Soy Sauce and Mayo Ⓜ

1 serving

1 to 2 pieces thinly sliced pork, about 2 oz (50 g)

1 serving cooked udon noodles

Pinch of shio kombu, or crazy salt

1 green onion (scallion), chopped

1 Tbsp mayo

½ Tbsp soy sauce

1. Cut the pork into bite-size pieces. Cut out a 12 inch (30 cm) square of kitchen parchment paper, and place the udon noodles in the middle. Spread the pork slices on top, and sprinkle with the shio kombu. Add the green onion, mayo and soy sauce in that order, and wrap the kitchen parchment paper around, twisting both ends closed like a candy wrapper.

2. Place the packet on a microwave-safe plate. Microwave on the high setting for 4 minutes. Open up the packet and mix everything well.

* I use frozen precooked udon noodles, defrosted overnight in the refrigerator. Try any type of precooked noodles or pasta instead.

*Thanks for cutting the noodles into easy-to-eat pieces for me, Mom!
—My daughter Naa*

This was great!
—*My son,
Tenkichi*

## Chicken with Mayo and Citrus Sauce

**1 serving**
½ skinless chicken thigh
Salt and pepper, to taste
1 Tbsp sake
Flour, for dusting
Vegetable oil, for cooking
1 Tbsp mayo
1 Tbsp ponzu sauce

1. Cut the chicken into bite-size diagonal slices. Sprinkle with the salt, pepper and sake, and dust with flour.

2. Heat the oil in a frying pan, put in the chicken in one layer and cook until browned on both side

3. Wipe out any excess oil from the frying pan using paper towels. Add the mayo and ponzu sauce and mix to coat the chicken.

Side

Side

Main

## Root Vegetable Salad

**2–3 servings**
1 carrot, or ½ burdock root
1 tsp sesame oil
1 Tbsp mentsuyu sauce
1 Tbsp rice vinegar
3 tablespoons water
1 Tbsp mayo

1. Cut the carrot into thin diagonal slices, then shred finely and briefly place in a bowl of cold water. Drain well.

2. Put the carrot and sesame oil in a pan and turn on the heat. Stir-fry briefly. Add the mentsuyu, rice vinegar and water, and cook while stirring occasionally until no moisture is left in the pan. When the carrot is cooked through, turn the heat off, take out of the pan and leave until cool. Mix with the mayo.

## Celery and Egg Salad

**1 serving**
½ celery stalk, roughly chopped
Salt, for sprinkling
1 hard-boiled egg
1 Tbsp mayo
½ tsp karashi mustard or English mustard
Salt and pepper, to taste

1. Sprinkle the celery with a little salt. When the celery has softened, squeeze it tightly to eliminate excess moisture.

2. Mash up the egg with a fork, and mix with the celery. Add the mayo, mustard, and salt and pepper and mix well.

* Try adding ume paste or a chopped up umeboshi plum instead of the mustard.

## Sautéed Salmon & Mayo

**1 serving**
4 oz (100 g) fresh salmon
Salt and pepper, to taste
Cornstarch, for dusting
Vegetable oil, for cooking
1 Tbsp mayo
1 Tbsp ketchup
1 Tbsp maple syrup

1. Cut the salmon into bite-size pieces. Season with salt and pepper and dust with cornstarch.

2. Heat the oil in a frying pan. Put in the salmon in one layer, and fry while turning occasionally until cooked through.

3. Mix the mayo, ketchup and maple syrup, and add to the pan. Mix to coat the salmon.

# Pumpkin and Bacon Salad Ⓜ

1 serving

¾ cup (100 g) deseeded kabocha or butternut squash
Pinch of salt
1 slice bacon, cut into small strips
1 Tbsp mayo
½ tsp karashi mustard or English mustard

1. Cut the squash into bite-size pieces, and put in a microwave-safe container skin side down. Sprinkle with salt and scatter with the bacon. Cover loosely with cling film.
2. Microwave on the high setting for 2½ minutes until a skewer goes through easily. Add the mayo and mustard and mix.

* This can also be made with sweet potato.

This eggplant was dangerous! In a good way! —*My daughter Naa*

Side

# Miso-Mayo Eggplant

1 serving

2 oz (50 g) eggplant
1 Tbsp mayo
1 tsp miso

1. Cut up the eggplant roughly and put the pieces in bowl of salted water. Soak for 10 minutes, then drain well.

2. Put the mayo and eggplant in a frying pan. Mix well before turning on the heat. Cook over medium-low heat.

3. When the eggplant is soft, add the miso, turn off the heat, and mix well.

Side

● Seasoned with Mayo ●

Side

# Seafood and Mushroom Stir-Fry

1 serving

1 cup (100 g) frozen seafood mix
Handful shimeji mushrooms, or mushrooms of your choice
Salt and pepper, to taste
1 Tbsp mayo
½ Tbsp soy sauce
Handful bonito flakes, optional

1. Rinse the surface ice off the seafood under cold running water. Drain in a colander. Cut the stem ends off the shimeji mushrooms and divide into small clumps.

2. Put the seafood in a small pan, sprinkle with salt and pepper, add the mayo and turn on the heat. Cook while coating the seafood with the mayo. When the seafood is cooked, add the mushrooms and continue cooking until the mushrooms are limp. Add the soy sauce and mix. Sprinkle with the bonito flakes and turn off the heat.

# Tangy Potato Salad Ⓜ

1 serving

1 medium potato
3 green beans
1 Tbsp mayo
1 tsp yukari shiso salt or crazy salt

1. Peel the potato and cut into bite-size pieces. Rinse briefly. Remove the strings and cut both ends off the green beans, and cut into ¾ inch (2 cm) lengths. Put the potato and green beans in a microwave-safe container and cover loosely with cling film. Microwave on the high setting for about 2½ minutes.

2. When a bamboo skewer goes through the potato easily, add the mayo and yukari and mix well.

* You can use sugar snap peas or green bell pepper instead of the green beans. Since they're just added for color, you can leave out the green vegetables if you want.

# Seasoned with Tomato Ketchup

Ketchup adds sweet, sour and savory flavors, and the red color can really brighten up a bento box!

## Savory Pork and Onions

1 serving

4 thin slices pork, about 4 oz (100 g)
¼ onion, cut into wedges
1 Tbsp mayo
1 Tbsp ketchup
Salt and pepper, to taste
1 tsp soy sauce
Vegetable oil, for cooking

1. Cut the pork into 4 pieces each. Put in a bowl with the onion, mayo, ketchup, salt, pepper and soy sauce, and mix. Heat the oil in a frying pan. Stir-fry the mix over medium-low heat taking care not to burn.

## Cheesy Ketchup Pumpkin

1 serving

4 thin slices kabocha or butternut squash
Salt, to taste
1 tsp olive oil
Shredded cheese, to taste
Ketchup, to taste

1. Put the squash slices in one layer on a sheet of foil. Sprinkle with salt and olive oil.

2. Wrap the foil around the squash to form a packet. Cook under a preheated grill for 6 minutes. Open the foil and top with cheese and ketchup while the squash is still hot. Let the cheese to melt with residual heat.

*This can be made with sliced potato too.

## Teriyaki Salmon

1 serving

4 oz (100 g) fresh salmon
Salt and pepper, to taste
1 Tbsp ketchup
1 tsp honey

1. Season the salmon with salt and pepper. Put on a sheet of foil. Coat with the ketchup and honey, and form a packet with the foil.

2. Put the foil packet under a preheated grill, and cook for 6 to 7 minutes.

* Add sliced onions to the foil packet to make this a heartier side for your bento.

## Chopped Pork Patties

1 serving

3 to 4 slices thinly sliced pork, about 4 oz (100 g), roughly chopped
Salt and pepper, to taste
1 Tbsp dried breadcrumbs
1 Tbsp ready-made fried onion
1 Tbsp mayo
¼ onion, thinly sliced
1 Tbsp ketchup
1 Tbsp tonkatsu sauce

1. Form a patty with the pork. Add the salt, pepper, breadcrumbs, fried onions and mayo, and mix together. Put the onion slices on a sheet of foil. Add the ketchup and tonkatsu sauce and turn the onion slices to coat. Top with the pork patty. Wrap up in the foil. Cook under a preheated grill for 10 minutes.

## Crunchy Lotus Root

1 serving

2 oz (50 g) lotus root, peeled
2 tsps ketchup
1 tsp mentsuyu sauce

1. Cut the lotus root into batons. Put into a bowl of water briefly. Drain.

2. Put the lotus root on a sheet of aluminum foil. Add the ketchup and mentsuyu and mix briefly to coat the lotus root. Wrap the foil around to form a packet.

3. Preheat the grill. Grill the foil packet for 7 minutes. Leave to cool in the closed packet.

## Chili Chicken

1 serving

½ large chicken breast
Salt and pepper, to taste
1 Tbsp flour
1 Tbsp ketchup
¼ tsp doubanjiang, optional
½ tsp sesame oil
1 tsp honey
Vegetable oil, for cooking

1. Cut the chicken into thin diagonal slices. Sprinkle with salt and pepper. Put the chicken and flour in a plastic bag and shake to coat the chicken. Mix the ketchup, doubanjiang, sesame oil and honey on a small plate.

2. Heat the oil in a frying pan. Put in the chicken in one layer and brown on both sides. When cooked, put it on the small plate from Step 1 and turn to coat with the sauce.

Side

## Fluffy Egg with Ketchup
**1 serving**  Ⓜ
**1 egg; 1 Tbsp mayo**
**1 tsp milk**
**1 slice processed cheese, chopped up**
**1 tsp ketchup**

1. Break the egg into a microwave-safe bowl. Add the mayo and milk and beat with a fork.

2. Put the cheese in the bowl on top of the egg. Cover loosely with cling film and microwave on the high setting for 1 to 1½ mins. Top with the ketchup.

* Delicious served on top of chicken and rice.

Side

## Tofu with Ketchup Ⓖ
**1 serving**
**½ abura-age tofu pouch, cut in strips**
**¼ onion, cut into wedges**
**1 tsp olive oil**
**1 Tbsp ketchup**
**½ tsp grainy mustard**
**½ tsp soy sauce**

1. Put the tofu and onion on a piece of foil. Drizzle on the olive oil. Wrap the foil around to form a packet.

2. Put the foil packet under a preheated grill for 5 minutes. Add the ketchup, mustard and soy sauce and mix well.

Main

## Stir-Fried Beef
**1 serving**
**3 to 4 pieces thinly sliced beef**
**Salt and pepper, to taste**
**Vegetable oil, for cooking**
**¼ onion, thinly sliced**
**1 Tbsp ketchup**
**½ Tbsp oyster sauce**
**Chopped parsley for garnish**

1. Cut the beef into bite-size pieces and season with the salt and pepper.

2. Heat the oil in a frying pan, and stir-fry the onion and beef. When the onion has softened, season with the ketchup and oyster sauce, and sprinkle with parsley.

Main

## Chicken & Green Beans
**1 serving**
**2 chicken tenders, sinew removed**
**Salt and pepper, to taste**
**Cornstarch, for dusting**
**Vegetable oil, for cooking**
**5 green beans, trimmed**
**2 tsps butter**
**1 Tbsp ketchup**
**½ Tbsp grated cheese**

1. Halve each chicken tender lengthwise. Season with salt and pepper, and dust with cornstarch.

2. Heat the oil in a frying pan, add the chicken and green beans in one layer, and pan-fry till browned. Add the butter, ketchup and cheese and mix. Turn off the heat.

* This can burn easily, so be sure to lower the heat before adding the flavoring ingredients.

Side

## Mushrooms with Ketchup
**1 serving**  Ⓜ
**2 king oyster mushrooms**
**1 tsp ketchup**
**1 tsp mentsuyu sauce**

1. Cut the mushrooms into bite-size pieces. Place in a microwave-safe container and cover loosely with cling film. Microwave on the high setting for 90 seconds.

2. Add the ketchup and mentsuyu and mix well. Leave to cool.

* Try this with shimeji, buna shimeji (white shimeji), enoki or other types of mushrooms.

Side

## Cabbage Omelet
**1 serving**
**2 cabbage leaves**
**1 egg**
**Pinch of salt**
**Pinch of sugar**
**Vegetable oil**
**Ketchup, to taste**

This one is really tasty.
—*My daughter Naa*

1. Put the cabbage in a microwave-safe container and cover loosely with cling film. Microwave on the high setting for 1 minute. Squeeze the cabbage leaves to remove excess moisture, and slice thinly. Put in a bowl with the egg, salt and sugar. Mix well.

2. Heat up a rectangular tamagoyaki pan (see page 90 for how to make in a regular frying pan) and spread with vegetable oil. Add half the egg and cabbage mixture over about half the bottom of the tamagoyaki pan (my pan measures about 3 inches x 5 inches [8 cm x 12 cm]) and cook until browned on the bottom. Turn and brown the other side too.

3. Cut up and decorate with ketchup.

# Seasoned with Pickled Plum

Umeboshi pickled plum is a classic bento ingredient with a tangy taste that's addictive! Use whole, chopped, or in ready-made paste form, from Japanese grocery stores or online.

## Chicken in Plum Sauce Ⓖ

1 serving

1 boneless, skinless chicken thigh
Salt, to taste
2 tsps mentsuyu sauce
⅓ umeboshi pickled plum, chopped
Chopped green onion (scallion), for garnish

1. Pound the thick parts of the chicken to flatten. Cut diagonally into bite-size pieces. Season with salt, and let rest for 10 minutes.

2. Put a foil sheet under a grill. Put the chicken on it in one layer. Cook for 7 minutes.

3. Mix the mentsuyu, umeboshi and green onion. Put the cooked chicken in the sauce while still hot, and leave to cool. Garnish with the green onion.

## Cabbage & Plum Salad

1 serving

1 to 2 cabbage leaves
Salt, to taste
⅓ umeboshi pickled plum, pitted
1 tsp olive oil

1. Cut the cabbage into fairly small pieces. Place in a bowl and sprinkle with the salt. Squeeze excess moisture from the cabbage until it turns limp.

2. Tear the umeboshi flesh into small pieces. Add to the cabbage with the olive oil and mix.

* Try sesame oil instead of olive oil.

## Zingy Spinach & Cheese

1 serving

1 slice processed cheese
¼ cup (50 g) blanched and squeezed-out spinach (see page 11)
⅓ umeboshi pickled plum
1 tsp mentsuyu sauce

1. Cut the cheese into small dice.

2. Cut the spinach and place in a bowl with the cheese. Remove the pit from the umeboshi and cut up the fruit part. Add to the spinach and cheese with the mentsuyu and mix.

## Chicken Piccata

2 servings

2 large chicken tenders
Salt, pepper, and flour for sprinkling
1 umeboshi pickled plum, pitted
1 egg
2 green shiso leaves, chopped
Vegetable oil, for cooking

1. Butterfly each chicken tender by slicing horizontally, then opening up into a thin large piece. Cut into 3 so you end up with 6 pieces. Sprinkle with salt and pepper and flour. Tear the flesh of the umeboshi into small pieces. Mix the egg, umeboshi and shiso in a bowl. Put the chicken in the egg mixture and coat.

2. Heat the oil in a frying pan. Put in chicken pieces in one layer. Brown on both sides. Add any leftover egg mixture it as it cooks.

## Plum & Soy Mackerel Ⓖ

1 serving

1 piece mackerel
Salt, to taste
A little sake
½ umeboshi pickled plum, pitted
1 tsp soy sauce
½ tsp grated ginger

1. Sprinkle the fish with salt and sake, and let rest for 10 mins. Pat dry with paper towels. Put the fish on a piece of foil, and cook under a preheated grill for 6 minutes.

2. Tear the umeboshi plum into pieces. Put the cooked fish on a plate and coat with the plum, soy sauce and ginger. Leave until cool.

## Zesty Chicken Sauté

1 serving

1 boneless, skinless chicken breast
Salt and pepper, to taste
1 Tbsp flour
1 umeboshi pickled plum, pitted
2 tsps ponzu sauce
Vegetable oil, for cooking

1. Cut the chicken into thin diagonal slices, and sprinkle with salt and pepper.

2. Put the chicken and the flour into a plastic bag, and shake to coat the chicken. Chop the umeboshi into a paste. Combine the ponzu sauce and umeboshi in a small bowl.

3. Heat up some vegetable oil in a frying pan and put the chicken in in a single layer. Cook until browned on both sides. Add to the bowl from Step 2 and mix to coat with the sauce.

## Chicken & Plum Patties

**Makes 4 patties** Ⓖ

⅔ cup (150 g) ground chicken
½ umeboshi pickled plum, pitted
1 Tbsp mayo
1 Tbsp cornstarch
Salt and pepper, to taste
A little sesame oil
A little chopped green onion (scallion)

1. Put the chicken, chopped umeboshi flesh, mayo, cornstarch, and salt and pepper in a bowl. Mix and divide into 4 equal portions. Form each into patties.

2. Brush the oil onto a sheet of foil, and put on the patties in a single layer. Wrap around the foil to form a packet. Grill for 9 mins. Garnish with the green onion.

## Omelet with Plum

**2 servings**

2 eggs
Handful bonito flakes, optional
½ umeboshi pickled plum, pitted
1 Tbsp chopped green onion (scallion)
A little salt
½ tsp soy sauce
2 Tbsps water
Vegetable oil, for cooking

1. Beat all ingredients except the oil in a bowl.

2. Heat the oil in a tamagoyaki pan (see page 90 for alternative). Add ⅓ of the egg mixture to the pan, and start rolling it up from the far side (see Japanese Omelet, page 19). Repeat 2 times until you have a three-layer rolled omelet.

## Potato Namul with Plum

**1 serving** Ⓜ

1 medium potato, peeled and shredded
1 tsp sesame oil
⅓ umeboshi pickled plum, chopped
A few drops vegetable stock
1 tsp ground sesame seeds

1. Rinse the potato in water, drain well and put in a microwave-safe container.

2. Sprinkle with the oil, cover loosely with cling film and microwave on the high setting for 2 minutes.

3. Add the umeboshi, stock and sesame seeds and mix.

* Namul is a Korean vegetable side dish.

## Cheesy Pork Rolls

**1 serving**

4 thin slices pork, about 4 oz (100 g)
1 slice processed cheese, cut in strips
Salt, pepper and flour for sprinkling
½ umeboshi pickled plum, pitted
1 tsp mirin
1 tsp soy sauce
1 tsp water
½ tsp grated ginger
Vegetable oil, for cooking

1. Spread out the pork slices, place some cheese on each slice and roll up tightly. Sprinkle with salt, pepper and flour. Chop the umeboshi flesh. Mix the umeboshi, mirin, soy sauce, water and ginger.

2. Heat the oil in a frying pan. Put in the pork and cheese rolls seam side down. Cook until browned while rolling around occasionally.

3. Add the sauce from Step 1, and turn the rolls so that they are coated in the sauce.

## Eggplant in Plum Sauce

**1 serving**

2 oz (50 g) eggplant
½ umeboshi pickled plum
2 tsps ponzu sauce

1. Cut the eggplant into fairly small pieces, Put some salt into a bowl of water and add the eggplant. Leave to soak for about a minute. Drain well.

2. Mix the eggplant, the ripped up fruit part of the umeboshi and ponzu sauce together.

* Try adding a little rice vinegar for extra oomph.

## Stir-Fried Plum Noodles

**1 serving** Ⓜ

½ baby leek, cut in 2 in (5 cm) pieces
1 serving cooked Chinese noodles
1 to 2 pieces thinly sliced pork, about 2 oz (50 g)
Salt and pepper, to taste
½ umeboshi pickled plum, pitted and shredded
1 teaspoon sesame oil
A few drops of vegetable stock

1. Shred the leek pieces thinly. Put the noodles on a 12" (30cm) square of parchment paper. Top with the leek, then the pork. Sprinkle with the salt, pepper, umeboshi, sesame oil and stock. Wrap the paper into a bundle and twist the ends closed. Microwave on the high setting for 3½ mins. When the meat is cooked, mix well.

The spicy aromas and flavors of curry really whet your appetite!

(Main)

(Side)

(Main)

## Curried Grilled Salmon

1 serving  (G)

4 oz (100 g) fresh salmon
Salt, to taste
½ tsp curry powder

1. Sprinkle the salmon evenly with salt and curry powder. Leave to rest for 5 minutes.

2. Place a sheet of foil under a preheated grill, and place the salmon on it. Cook for about 5 minutes, or until the salmon is done.

* Try cod, mackerel, or amberjack instead.

## Buttery Spinach & Corn

1 serving  (M)

¼ cup (50 g) blanched and squeezed-out spinach (see page 11)
1 Tbsp frozen sweet corn kernels
Salt, to taste
¼ tsp curry powder
1 tsp butter

1. Cut the spinach into short lengths. Put spinach and corn in a microwave-safe container, sprinkle with salt and curry powder, top with the butter and cover loosely with cling film. Microwave on the high setting for about 90 seconds. Mix well.

## Curried Pork with Green Beans

1 serving

5 green beans, trimmed
4 thin slices pork, about 4 oz (100 g)
½ tsp curry powder
2 tsps soy sauce
1 tsp olive oil

1. Bring a pan of water to a boil. Boil the green beans for 2 mins. Cut the pork into bite-size pieces. Add the pork to the water and cook until it changes color. Drain, rinsing the pork under cold water to wash off the surface fat. Pat dry with paper towels. Mix the curry powder, soy sauce and olive oil. Add the pork and green beans and mix well.

(Main)

(Sub)

(Main)

## Stir-Fried Curried Pork

1 serving

3 to 4 pieces thinly sliced pork, about 4 oz (100 g)
½ onion, thinly sliced
Vegetable oil, for cooking
Handful bonito flakes, optional
1 tsp sugar
2 tsps soy sauce
½ tsp curry powder

1. Cut the pork into bite-size pieces.

2. Heat up some vegetable oil in a frying pan, add the onion and stir-fry until limp. Add the pork and stir-fry until it changes color. Put in the sugar, soy sauce and curry powder and continue cooking until there is no moisture left in the pan. Finish by sprinkling with bonito flakes.

* This is great made with beef too.

## Curry-Marinated Carrot

2 servings

1 medium carrot
1 tsp raisins
Salt, to taste
¼ tsp curry powder
½ tsp honey
1 tsp olive oil

1. Cut the carrot into thin diagonal slices, then shred finely. Put into a bowl. Add the raisins, salt, curry powder, honey and olive oil and mix. Cover tightly with cling film and leave to rest for 10 minutes.

## Honey Teriyaki Chicken

1 serving

1 boneless skinless chicken breast
Salt and pepper, to taste
1 Tbsp flour
Vegetable oil, for cooking
A little curry powder
1 tsp honey
1 tsp soy sauce

1. Cut the chicken diagonally into pieces, and sprinkle with salt and pepper.

2. Put the chicken and flour in a plastic bag, and shake well to coat the chicken. Combine the curry powder, honey and soy sauce.

3. Heat the oil in a frying pan. Put in the chicken in one layer, and brown on both sides. When cooked, pour in the combined flavoring ingredients from Step 2, turn off the heat and turn the chicken to coat in the sauce and make it shiny.

This is so good with rice!
—*My daughter Naa*

**Side**

**Main**

## Curried Chicken ⑤

**Makes 4 patties**

1 boneless skinless chicken thigh
Salt, to taste
½ tsp curry powder
2 tsps mentsuyu sauce
A little chopped green onion (scallion)

1. Slice the chicken horizontally, then open up to form a large thin piece. Slice into pieces, and sprinkle with salt. Let rest for 10 minutes.

2. Preheat the grill. Line a grill pan with aluminum foil. Put the chicken pieces on the foil and cook for about 7 minutes.

3. Combine the curry powder and mentsuyu in a bowl. Put in the chicken while still hot, and turn to coat with the sauce. Sprinkle with some chopped green onion and leave to cool.

**Main**

## Crispy Curried Chicken

**1 serving**

2 chicken tenders, sinew removed
½ tsp curry powder
1 tsp mayo
½ tsp soy sauce
Salt, to taste
Cornstarch, for dusting
Vegetable oil, for cooking

1. Cut the chicken in bite-size pieces. Mix curry powder, mayo, soy sauce, and salt. Coat the chicken with it. Dust with cornstarch.

2. Heat a good amount of oil in a frying pan. Drop the chicken pieces in the hot oil one at a time, and shallow fry until golden brown.

## Spicy Buttered Pumpkin

**2 servings**

1 cup (150 g) deseeded kabocha or
    butternut squash
Salt, to taste
1 tsp sugar
½ tsp curry powder
½ cup (125 ml) water
1 tsp soy sauce
2 tsps butter

1. Cut the squash into 1 inch (2.5 cm) pieces. Put in a small pan skin side down. Add salt, sugar, curry powder, water and soy sauce, partially cover with a lid and bring to a boil over medium heat. Simmer till the squash is cooked. Add the butter at the end, and turn the squash pieces to coat with the butter.

**Side**

## Curried Noodles Ⓜ

**1 serving**

2 thin slices pork, about 2 oz (50 g)
5 green beans, trimmed
Precooked frozen udon noodles
Salt and pepper
½ tsp curry powder
1 tsp soy sauce
1 tsp sesame oil

1. Cut the pork into bite-size pieces. Cut the green beans into 1 inch (2.5 cm) pieces.

2. Put the noodles on a 12 inch (30 cm) piece square parchment paper. Put the green beans then the pork on top. Sprinkle with salt, pepper and curry powder. Drizzle with soy sauce and sesame oil, and wrap the paper into a bundle, twisting both ends closed. Microwave for 4 minutes on the high setting. When cooked, open and mix well.

## Curried Onion Tempura

**1 serving**

½ onion, thinly sliced
½ tsp curry powder; pinch of salt
3 Tbsps flour
1 Tbsp water
Vegetable oil, for cooking

1. Put the onion, curry powder, salt and flour in a bowl. Mix well to coat the onion. Add the water and mix a few times.

2. Put a generous amount of oil in a frying pan and heat. Divide the onion-batter mixture into 3 portions, and drop them one at a time into the hot oil. Shallow fry until browned on both sides. Repeat with the rest of the batter.

**Side**

## Curried Cheese Omelet

I really love this!
—*My daughter Sue*

**1 serving**

1 egg
Pinch of salt
1 tsp sugar
½ tsp curry powder
½ tsp soy sauce
2 Tbsps water
1 slice processed cheese, diced
Vegetable oil, for cooking

1. Mix everything but the oil in a bowl.

2. Spread some vegetable oil in a tamagoyaki pan (see page 90 for alternative) and heat the pan. Add the egg mixture in 3 batches (see Japanese Omelet, page 19), sprinkling in some of the cheese after each batch is poured into the pan. Roll up the egg, and add another third of the egg. Sprinkle with cheese again and roll up. Repeat once more.

3. Slice into easy-to-eat pieces.

# Salads and Sweet Touches

To prevent sweet dishes and salads from becoming contaminated by other food in the bento box, be sure to pack them in separate containers.

## Stir-Fried Seafood

1 serving

1 cup (100 g) frozen seafood mix
1 Tbsp olive oil
½ yellow or red bell pepper, diced
1 Tbsp white wine vinegar
A pinch of salt and black pepper
½ tsp sugar
½ onion, thinly sliced
1 tsp lemon juice
Dried herbs of your choice, to taste

1. Put the seafood in a colander. Rinse off surface ice under cold water. Drain well.

2. Put the seafood in a small pan, add the olive oil, cover the pan with a lid and put on the heat. When heated through, mix it up and add the bell pepper, wine vinegar, salt, pepper and sugar and cook over high heat until there is no moisture left in the pan. Add the onion, mix and turn off the heat.

3. Add the lemon juice and dried herbs, and leave until cool.

## Sweet Orange and Tomato

2 servings

1 medium orange
1 small tomato
1 tsp lemon juice
1 tsp maple syrup
Salt, to taste

1. Cut the orange and tomato into ¾ inch (2 cm) pieces. Put both into a bowl, add the lemon juice, maple syrup and salt, and mix. Cover the bowl tightly with cling film and leave to rest for 10 minutes.

## Marinated Strawberries

2 servings

1 cup (150 g) hulled strawberries
2 tsps maple syrup
1 tsp white wine vinegar

1. Cut the strawberries in half if they are big. Sprinkle with the maple syrup and vinegar, and leave to rest for 10 minutes or so.

* Delicious made with cherry tomatoes instead of strawberries.

## Kiwi and Carrot Salad

1 serving

1 small carrot, finely shredded
½ kiwi fruit, sliced into half rounds
Pinch of salt
1 tsp lemon juice
1 tsp maple syrup
1 tsp extra virgin olive oil

1. Put all ingredients in a bowl and mix a few times. Put a piece of cling film directly on top of the contents of the bowl, and leave to rest for about 10 minutes.

* Try with orange instead of kiwi.

## Potato and Apple Salad

**1 serving**
⅔ cup (100 g) diced sweet potato
¼ apple
½ cup (125 ml) water
1 tsp marmalade
¼ tsp salt
1 tsp sugar
2 tsps lemon juice

1. Rinse the sweet potato under cold water. Cut up the apple to about the same size.

2. Put all ingredients in a small pan over medium heat. Simmer until the sweet potato is cooked through and there is very little moisture left in the pan, about 10 minutes.

## Grapefruit and Celery Salad

**2 servings**
½ celery stalk
Salt, for sprinkling
1 grapefruit
2 tsps extra virgin olive oil
Black pepper, to taste

1. Cut the celery into thin diagonal slices. Place in a bowl, sprinkle with some salt and leave to rest until the celery is limp. Squeeze tightly to eliminate extra moisture. (Don't rinse off the salt.) Peel the grapefruit and take out the fruit from the sacs.

2. Combine the celery and grapefruit, add the olive oil and black pepper, and mix.

## Crunchy Coleslaw

**1 serving**
1 large cabbage leaf
A small piece of carrot, shredded
Salt, to taste
½ tsp maple syrup
1 tsp lemon juice
1 Tbsp mayo
Black pepper, to taste

1. Cut the cabbage into ½-inch (1 cm) strips. Put in a bowl with the carrot, sprinkle with salt and rub it in. When the vegetables are limp, squeeze to eliminate extra moisture.

2. Add the maple syrup, lemon juice, mayo and black pepper, and mix well.

* The carrot is added for color, so you can leave it out if you like. Or add some corn kernels instead or in addition to the carrot.

## "Sweet" Potato Salad

**2 servings**
½ sweet potato, peeled
1 Tbsp raisins
Salt, to taste
1 tsp maple syrup
1 tsp lemon juice
1 Tbsp mayo

1. Cut the potato up roughly and rinse briefly. Put in a pan with salted cold water to cover. Bring to a boil and cook.

2. When a skewer goes through the sweet potato easily, drain, return the potato to the pan and shake the pan around to evaporate the moisture. Add the raisins, salt, maple syrup and lemon juice and mix. Let cool, then mix in the mayo.

* Add cream cheese for a tasty twist.

## Apple & Cabbage Salad

**1 serving**
1 large cabbage leaf
¼ apple, thinly sliced
Salt, to taste
½ tsp grainy mustard
1 tsp extra virgin olive oil
1 tsp lemon juice

1. Cut the cabbage into 1-inch (2½ cm) square pieces. Slice the apple thinly and cut to about the same size as the cabbage.

2. Sprinkle the cabbage with salt, rub it in, and squeeze tightly to eliminate extra moisture. Put the cabbage in a bowl.

3. Add the apple, mustard, olive oil and lemon juice to the bowl and mix.

## Honey Nut Squash Salad

**2 servings**
¾ cup (100 g) deseeded kabocha or
    butternut squash, cubed
2 Tbsps walnuts
2 oz (50 g) chilled cream cheese
Salt, to taste
2 tsps honey

1. Put the squash in a pan with salted cold water to cover. Turn on the heat, bring to a boil and cook. Chop the walnuts roughly, and cut the cream cheese into small dice.

2. When a skewer goes easily through the squash, drain, return to the pan and shake to evaporate any excess moisture. Leave to cool a bit, then mix in the other ingredients.

* This can be made with sweet potato too.

## My Daughter Naa's Bentos

Naa's school bag has an amazing number of food mascots hanging from it. There's an impressively realistic, wobbly silicone replica of a fried egg, a very fresh—or rather, fresh-looking—sweet shrimp sashimi, a piece of crisply fried pumpkin tempura, a juicy tomato wedge, a chicken wing that seems to be dripping with sweet and savory sauce, and a piece of grilled, salted salmon that looks as though it's crying out to be eaten with a bowl of rice.

Since she participates in a sport at school that requires her to keep strict control of her weight, she has to constantly watch the scales and pay attention to everything she puts in her mouth. That means she's always starving—or at least, to me it seems that way—don't you feel hungry all the time when you are watching what you eat? Maybe that's why she has so many realistic looking food mascots, even though they are just toys . . . In fact, she says that she always gets hungry sometime around eleven in the morning, so she gazes at her food samples and imagines she's eating them. Apparently, she spends the morning thinking "One more hour to go, just one more hour to go, then I can eat the bento Mom made for me this morning, just one more hour, c'mon, it's almost bento time . . ."

"So, that's why," my daughter says to me emphatically, "That's why, you have to make me delicious bentos, please Mom! I don't want to eat sad bentos! I just want to eat really yummy bentos! I look forward to my bentos that much, do you understand?"

Next year, Naa is going to graduate from middle school and go on to high school. I'll be making her bentos for at least three more years. And maybe after that too . . .

# CHAPTER 2

# Time-Saving Techniques

In this chapter, I'll introduce some tips and tricks to cut down on the time needed to make bentos. If you use them, you too will be able to make bentos easily in just ten minutes in the morning!

Rule 1: Make 3 items at once in the microwave!

Rule 2: Grill 3 items at the same time!

Rule 3: Marinate dishes so they "cook" while you sleep!

Rule 4: Use thermos food jars!

Rule 5: Make on the weekends, just pack on weekdays!

**Rule 1**

**Make 3 items at once in the microwave!**

If you make three items at once in a microwave oven, you can really cut down on bento prep time. Some things are seasoned before microwaving, and some things are seasoned afterwards, but either way, since everything is made by wrapping in cling film or kitchen parchment paper, there's no washing up to do.

These peppers are so juicy!
—*My daughter Naa*

# Stuffed Pepper Bento

*You won't believe how good these microwaved dishes taste!*

## Stuffed Bell Peppers

1 serving

2 small or 1 medium bell pepper
Flour, for dusting
½ cup (100 g) ground chicken
1 Tbsp dried breadcrumbs
1 Tbsp mayo
1 tsp oyster sauce
Salt and pepper, to taste
White sesame seeds, for garnish

1. Halve the peppers, deseed, and dust the insides with flour. Mix the chicken with the breadcrumbs, mayo, oyster sauce, salt and pepper.

2. Stuff the peppers with the chicken mixture. Put some sesame seeds on top of the meat. Put the peppers on kitchen paper, wrap and twist the ends closed.
** Go to the combined.

## Ratatouille

1 serving

1 oz (30 g) eggplant
3 cherry tomatoes
¼ onion
1 slice bacon
Pinch of salt
½ Tbsp extra virgin olive oil
Dried mixed herbs, to taste

1. Cut the eggplant roughly. Cut the cherry tomatoes in half, and the onion into thin wedges. Cut the bacon into ½ inch (1 cm) strips. Put all the ingredients on a sheet of kitchen parchment paper (see Photo 1), wrap tightly and twist the ends closed.

** Go to the combined.

## Sweet Potato with Lemon Butter

1 serving

Piece sweet potato, about
    4 oz (100 g)
1 tsp butter
1 tsp lemon juice
Salt, to taste

1. Slice the sweet potato into ¼ inch (6 mm) thick rounds. Rinse in cold water.

2. Wrap with cling film (see Photo 2).

** Go to the combined.

3. When the potato is cooked, mix in the butter, lemon juice and salt. (See Photo 4).

**Combined:**
** Put all three packets on a microwave-safe plate, and microwave on the high setting for 6 minutes.

## Tips

When seasoning ingredients before cooking, season them together on kitchen parchment paper.

To keep ingredients moist, wrap in cling film. (To keep drier, wrap in kitchen paper and twist closed.)

Put all three packets on a microwave-safe plate, and put the plate in the microwave.

When seasoning after cooking, spread out the wrapping, add the seasonings, and leave to cool.

# Ginger Salmon Bento
*Light and packed with vegetables*

## Ginger Salmon

1 serving

4 oz (100 g) fresh salmon
Salt and pepper, to taste
Flour, for dusting
1 tsp grated ginger
1 Tbsp mentsuyu sauce
1 tsp butter

1. Cut the salmon in half, season with salt and pepper and dust with flour.

2. Put the salmon on a sheet of kitchen parchment paper and spread with the ginger, mentsuyu and butter.

** Go to the combined.

## Mushrooms with Bonito Flakes

1 serving

Handful shimeji mushrooms, or mushrooms of your choice
1 king oyster mushroom
½ small packet bonito flakes
Salt, to taste

1. Cut the stem ends off the shimeji mushrooms and divide into small clumps. Cut the king oyster mushroom into bite-size pieces. Wrap both in cling film.

** Go to the combined.

2. When the mushrooms are cooked, open up the cling film and mix in the bonito flakes and salt.

## Citrusy Eggplant and Bell Pepper

1 serving

2 oz (50 g) eggplant
1 small bell pepper
1 tsp sesame oil
1 tsp ponzu sauce
Salt, to taste

1. Cut up the eggplant roughly. Deseed the bell pepper and cut up roughly. Wrap both in cling film.

** Go to the combined.

2. When the vegetables are cooked, mix with the sesame oil, ponzu sauce and salt.

Combined:
** Put all 3 packets on a microwave-safe plate, and microwave on the high setting for 5 minutes.

I love everything in this bento!
—*My daughter Naa*

# "Stir-fried" Pork and Bell Pepper Bento

*You can even stir-fry in a microwave!*

## Pork & Pepper "Stir-Fry"

**1 serving**
**4 thin slices pork, about 4 oz (100 g)**
**1 small bell pepper**
**1 tsp grated ginger**
**1 tsp mirin**
**1 tsp soy sauce**
**1 tsp cornstarch**
**1 tsp sesame oil**

**1.** Cut the pork and bell pepper into thin strips. Mix the pork with the ginger, mirin, soy sauce, cornstarch and sesame oil. Put the pork on a sheet of kitchen paper, put the pepper on top, wrap the paper up tightly and twist both ends closed.

** Go to the combined.

**2.** When cooked, mix well while separating the meat pieces.

Combined:
** Put all three packets on a microwave-safe plate, and microwave on the high setting for 5 minutes.

## Potato with Tuna

**1 serving**
**1 medium potato**
**2 Tbsps canned tuna**
**1 tsp mirin**
**1 tsp soy sauce**

**1.** Peel the potato and cut into 1 inch (2.5 cm) dice. Rinse in cold water and drain. Place the potato pieces on a sheet of kitchen parchment paper. Put the tuna on top and sprinkle with the mirin and soy sauce. Wrap the paper up tightly and twist both ends closed.

** Go to the combined.

## Celery with Mustard

**1 serving**
**¼ celery stalk**
**½ tsp karashi mustard or English mustard**
**Salt, to taste**
**1 tsp ground sesame seeds**

**1.** Cut up the celery roughly and wrap in cling film.

** Go to the combined.

**2.** When cooked, mix with the mustard, salt and sesame seeds.

*Rule 1* | Make 3 items at once in the microwave!

## Rule 2

### Grill 3 items at the same time!

As well as microwaving, one way to shorten cooking time is to use the grill function of your oven. When I want something nicely grilled and browned, or to bring out the sweetness in vegetables, it's the ideal cooking method. Preheat the grill beforehand and put the food to be cooked on foil, or wrap it up. Some dishes are seasoned before cooking, and some after, but the easy recipes here can all be cooked at once using the grill. Since everything is protected with foil, there's no cleanup to worry about either.

Pork and fried egg together is really delicious!
—*My daughter Sue*

# Sesame Pork and Fried Egg Bento

*Make both the pork and egg in one go using the grill!*

## Sesame Pork

**1 serving**
½ onion, thinly sliced
4 thinly slices pork, about 4 oz (100 g)
Salt and pepper, to taste
Splash of stock
1 tsp sesame oil
1 tsp ground sesame seeds
½ tsp karashi or English mustard

1. Line a sheet of foil with the onion. Spread the pork on top, sprinkle with salt and pepper, add the other ingredients and rub into the meat (see Photo 1). Wrap the foil around the food.

** Go to the combined.

## Fried Egg

**1 serving**
A little vegetable oil
1 egg

1. Brush a piece of aluminum foil that's been formed into a bowl with some vegetable oil, and break an egg onto the oiled foil. Cook the egg under the grill without closing up the foil.

** Go to the combined.

2. Take the egg out after 3 minutes.

## Asparagus and Bacon Salad

**1 serving**
3 asparagus stalks
1 slice bacon
1 tsp grainy mustard
1 tsp mayo

1. Peel the tough end of the asparagus stalk, and cut the stalk into thirds. Cut the bacon into ½ inch (1 cm) pieces.

2. Put the asparagus and bacon on foil, and wrap.

** Go to the combined.

3. Mix with the mustard and mayo after cooking (see Photo 4).

**Combined:**
** Put all three foil packets under the grill (see Photo 3), and cook under medium heat for 7 minutes. (Take the egg out after 3 minutes.)

## Tips

Aluminum foil with a nonstick coating is handy for this recipe. Alternatively, put some oil on regular foil.

When seasoning the ingredients before cooking, do it on top of the foil as shown.

The egg is cooked with the foil open like this. Anything that you want to get browned by the grill should be cooked with the foil open.

Both the closed and opened foil packets are grilled at the same time.

When seasoning the ingredients after cooking, put the flavoring ingredients on while the food is still hot and mix. Let cool.

# Crispy Chicken Bento
*The cheese-flavored breading is delicious!*

### Grilled Chicken Tenders

**1 serving**
2 chicken tenders, sinew removed
Salt and pepper, to taste
2 tsps mayo
1 tsp flour
2 Tbsps dried breadcrumbs
½ tsp grated cheese
2 tsps vegetable oil

**1.** Slice the chicken lengthwise in half to get 4 thin strips. Season with salt and pepper and coat with mayo and flour. Toss with the breadcrumbs and cheese. Sprinkle with the oil. Put the tenders on foil. Don't close the foil.   ** Go to the combined directions.

### Soy Sauce Mushrooms

**1 serving**
2 fresh shiitake mushrooms
Handful enoki mushrooms, or mushrooms of your choice
Handful bonito flakes, optional
1 tsp soy sauce

**1.** Cut the stem ends off the shiitake and enoki mushrooms. Cut into bite-size pieces, place on a piece of aluminum foil and wrap.

** Go to the combined directions.

**2.** When cooked, add the bonito flakes and soy sauce and mix.

### Cabbage and Wasabi Miso

**1 serving**
2 cabbage leaves
½ tsp miso
½ tsp wasabi paste
1 tsp mayo

**1.** Cut the cabbage into ¾ inch (2 cm) square pieces. Place on a piece of foil and wrap.

** Go to the combined directions.

**2.** When cooked, add the miso, wasabi and mayo and mix.

Combined directions:
** Put all 3 foil packets under the grill, and cook under medium heat for 7 minutes. Turn the chicken tenders over halfway through.

# Eggplant and Meat Patty Bento

*Yes, you can make a "boiled" egg using the grill!*

## Eggplant and Meat Patty

**1 serving**

**1 oz (30 g) eggplant**
**¼ cup (50 g) ground beef**
**¼ cup (50 g) ground pork**
**1 tsp miso**
**2 Tbsps dried breadcrumbs**
**Salt and pepper, to taste**

1. Cut the eggplant into small dice. Combine with all the other ingredients and mix well. Form into a round patty and place on a piece of aluminum foil.

**\*\* Go to the combined directions.**

## Grilled "Boiled" Egg

**1 serving**

**1 egg**
**Salt, to taste**

1. Make sure you are using an egg that's at room temperature. Wrap the egg in foil.

**\*\* Go to the combined directions.**

2. When cooked, leave for 10 minutes still wrapped in the foil, to allow it to continue cooking in the residual heat.

3. Peel, cut in half, and sprinkle with salt.

## Sweet & Sour Squash

**1 serving**

**Small piece kabocha or butternut**
**    squash, deseeded and sliced**
**1 tsp honey**
**Salt and curry powder, to taste**
**A few raisins**

1. Wrap the squash in foil.

**\*\* Go to the combined directions.**

2. Once grilled, mix with the other ingredients.

Rule 2 | Grill 3 items at the same time!!

**Combined directions:**
**\*\* Place all 3 foil packets under the grill, and cook under medium heat for 8 minutes.**

## Rule 3

### Marinate dishes so they "cook" while you sleep!

Just put the ingredients and seasonings in a plastic zip bag, refrigerate overnight, and one item is done. If you make these marinade bags while you're prepping dinner, it's a piece of cake!

**Tips**

**1** Put ingredients and seasonings in a zip bag.

**2** Squeeze and rub the bag to distribute the seasonings.

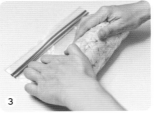

**3** With the bag still open, carefully push out any excess air from the bag.

**4** Zip up the bag with all the air eliminated from it.

## Marinated Cabbage

*Keeps 5 days refrigerated*

**4 servings**
3 cabbage leaves
Splash of vegetable stock
1 Tbsp rice vinegar

1. Cut the cabbage into bite size pieces.

2. Put all the ingredients into a plastic zip bag (see Tips, above). Refrigerate overnight.

* You can make this with napa or Chinese cabbage too. Add a little wasabi paste or yuzu kosho for a spicy accent.

## Lemon Daikon

*Keeps 5 days refrigerated*

**4 servings**
1 piece daikon radish, about 8 oz (250 g)
¼ lemon, thinly sliced
½ tsp salt
1 tsp sugar

1. Peel the daikon radish, cut into quarters and slice thinly.

2. Put all the ingredients into a plastic zip bag (see Tips, above). Refrigerate overnight.

* You can make this with tender young turnips too.

Keeps 5 days refrigerated

## Chinese Carrots

4 servings

1 large carrot
2 tsps sugar
1 Tbsp soy sauce
1 red Thai chili pepper
1 tsp sesame oil

1. Slice the carrot in half lengthwise, and then cut into thin slices.

2. Put all the ingredients into a plastic zip bag (see Tips, facing page). Refrigerate overnight.

Keeps 3 days refrigerated

## Ginger Cucumber

4 servings

2 small Japanese-style
   cucumbers
Salt for sprinkling
3 Tbsps mentsuyu sauce
2 tsps grated ginger
1 tsp sesame oil

1. Cut the cucumbers into batons. Sprinkle with the salt and leave until they turn a little limp. Squeeze out the excess moisture, put all the ingredients into a plastic zip bag (see Tips, facing page), and refrigerate overnight.

Keeps 3 days refrigerated

## Spicy Greens

2 servings

5 oz (150 g) komatsuna,
   turnip greens, or bok choy
Pinch of salt
1 tsp sugar
2 tsps soy sauce
2 tsps karashi mustard or English mustard

1. Cut the greens into 1½ inch (4cm) lengths.

2. Put all the ingredients into a plastic zip bag (see Tips, facing page). Refrigerate overnight.

Keeps 5 days refrigerated

## Sesame Sticks

4 servings

2 carrots, or 2 burdock roots
½ tsp salt
1 Tbsp sugar
1 Tbsp soy sauce
1 Tbsp rice vinegar
2 Tbsps ground sesame seeds

1. Peel the carrots (or scrape the skin off the burdock) and cut into 2 inch (5 cm) lengths. Rinse briefly.

2. Put the carrot in a pan of boiling water for 3 mins. Drain.

3. Put the carrot and the rest of the ingredients into a plastic zip bag (see Tips, facing page). Refrigerate overnight.

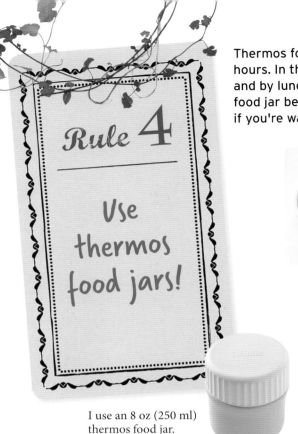

## Rule 4

### Use thermos food jars!

I use an 8 oz (250 ml) thermos food jar.

Thermos food jars keep their contents hot or cold for several hours. In the morning I put in the ingredients and boiling water and by lunchtime everything is cooked and ready to eat! Thermos food jar bentos are easy and healthy, and these reicpes are great if you're watching your weight. You'll find thermos food jars online.

*Tips*

Put all the ingredients in the thermos food jar . . .

Add boiling water, close the lid immediately and you're done! (After 5 hours the contents will gradually start to cool and eventually become lukewarm.)

## Noodle Soup with Plum

**1 serving**

Pinch of shio kombu
1 umeboshi pickled plum
1 tsp white
    sesame seeds
¼ oz (10g) glass noodles
Chopped green onion
    (scallion), to taste
¾ cup (185 ml) boiling
    water

1. Put all the ingredients in a thermos food jar, add boiling water and close the lid.

* I used precut noodles. If you have the long type, cut them into short pieces with kitchen scissors.

** Use crazy salt if you don't have shio kombu.

## Chinese Style Shrimp Soup

**1 serving**

1 tsp sakura shrimp
1 tsp dried, cut wakame
    seaweed, optional
1 tsp sesame oil
Chopped green onion
    (scallion), to taste
⅓ tsp salt
¾ cup (185 ml) boiling
    water

1. Put all the ingredients in a thermos food jar, add boiling water and close the lid.

## Hearty Cabbage Soup

**1 serving**

1 cabbage leaf
Splash of vegetable stock
1 tsp ground
   sesame seeds
1 tsp sesame oil
¾ cup (185 ml) boiling
   water

1. Cut the cabbage into bite-size pieces.

2. Put all the ingredients in a thermos food jar, add boiling water and close the lid.

## Tomato, Corn and Cheese Soup

**1 serving**

3 cherry tomatoes
1 Tbsp frozen sweet corn
Pinch of shio kombu
Black pepper, to taste
1 slice processed cheese
¾ cup (185 ml) boiling
   water

1. Cut the cherry tomatoes in half.

2. Put all the ingredients in a thermos food jar, add boiling water and close the lid.

*Use crazy salt if you don't have shio kombu.

## Mushroom and Onion Soup

**1 serving**

Small handful shimeji or
   other mushrooms
1 Tbsp fried onion*
Pinch of bonito flakes
½ tsp soy sauce
Pinch of salt
¾ cup (185 ml) boiling
   water

1. Cut the stem ends off the shimeji mushrooms, and divide into single mushrooms.

2. Put all the ingredients in a thermos food jar, add boiling water and close the lid.

*You can use ready-made fried onion.

## Macaroni Sweet Corn Soup

**1 serving**

1 Tbsp frozen corn
2 Tbsps quick cooking
   macaroni
1 Tbsp fried onion
½ tsp curry powder
Pinch of bonito flakes
¾ cup (185 ml) boiling
   water

1. Put all the ingredients in a thermos food jar, add boiling water and close the lid.

*Use ready-made fried onion.

# Rule 5

## Make on the weekends, just pack on weekdays!

Bento-making is easier if you prepare some items in advance and stash them in the fridge. Be sure to use clean containers and utensils to avoid spoilage.

## Super-Quick Chicken Ⓜ

**3 servings**

3 chicken tenders, sinew removed
Salt, pepper and sugar, to taste
1 Tbsp olive oil

1. Sprinkle the chicken on both sides with salt, pepper and sugar. Let rest for 15 minutes at room temperature.

2. Drizzle with olive oil, cover loosely with cling film and microwave on the high setting for 2 mins. Turn the chicken over and microwave for 1 min. Let rest with the cling film still on for 30 seconds.

3. Shred the chicken. Transfer to a storage container and refrigerate.

## Lotus Root in Oyster Sauce

**4 servings**

8 oz (250 g) lotus root, peeled
1 Tbsp sesame oil
1 Tbsp oyster sauce
1 tsp sugar
1 tsp soy sauce
1 tsp rice vinegar

1. Slice the lotus root thinly. Put in a bowl of cold water for a few minutes. Drain.

2. Heat the oil in a frying pan, add the lotus root and stir-fry until translucent. Add the oyster sauce, sugar, soy sauce and vinegar, and stir-frying until all moisture is gone. Cool, and store in the refrigerator.

## Korean Vegetables

**4 servings**

4 oz (100 g) beef offcuts
1 Tbsp sesame oil
1 carrot cut in matchsticks
1 burdock root cut in matchsticks (optional)
2 tsps sugar
2 tsps gochujang bean paste
1 tsp mirin
1 tsp soy sauce

1. Cut the beef into ½ inch (1 cm) pieces. Heat the oil in a frying pan, add the beef and stir-fry until it changes color. Add the veg and stir-fry until limp. Add the other ingredients, and stir-fry until no moisture is left in the pan. Cool, put in a storage container and refrigerate.

## Simmered Sweet Potato

**4 servings**

1 large sweet potato, about 12 oz (350 g)
¾ cup (185 ml) water
2 Tbsps sugar
½ tsp salt
½ tsp soy sauce

1. Cut the ends off the potatoes, and cut off strips of peel using a vegetable peeler. Cut into ½ inch (1 cm) thick slices. Put into a bowl of water for a few minutes. Drain.

2. Put the potatoes and water in a pan, add the sugar, salt and soy sauce and bring to a boil. Turn the heat to low, put a small lid directly on top of the pan's contents, and simmer for 12 to 13 minutes. Cool, transfer to a storage container and refrigerate.

## Marinated Mushrooms

**4 servings**

Large handful shimeji mushrooms
Large handful maitake mushrooms (or mushrooms of your choice)
1 Tbsp olive oil
2 slices bacon, finely chopped
Splash of vegetable stock
1 tsp grainy mustard
1 Tbsp white wine vinegar
A little grated garlic

1. Trim the mushrooms and cut into bite-size pieces. Heat the oil in a frying pan, and stir-fry the mushrooms until limp. Add the other ingredients and stir-fry for another minute. Turn off the heat. Cool, transfer to a storage container and refrigerate.

# Mushroom Medley

**4 servings**

Large handful maitake mushrooms
Large handful king oyster mushrooms
  (or mushrooms of your choice)
1 Tbsp mirin
1 Tbsp soy sauce
1 Tbsp sakura shrimp

1. Cut the mushrooms into bite-size pieces.

2. Put the mushrooms and all the other ingredients into a pan. Cook while stirring occasionally until the mushrooms have decreased in volume by half, and turned limp. Cool, transfer to a container and refrigerate.

# Bok Choy and Sesame Namul

**4 servings**

14 oz (400 g) bok choy
½ tsp salt
1 Tbsp sesame salt
1 Tbsp ground sesame seeds

1. Cut the bok choy into 1 inch (2.5 cm) pieces. Cut the bases into wedges. Put the bok choy in a pan of boiling salted water for a few minutes until it turns bright green. Drain, rinse and squeeze out.

2. Put the bok choy in a bowl, add the ½ tsp of salt, sesame salt and sesame seeds and mix well. Refrigerate.

# Simmered Fried Tofu

**4 servings**

4 abura-age tofu pouches
¾ cup (185 ml) water
2 Tbsps sugar
1 tsp soy sauce

1. Place the tofu pouches in a single layer in a colander and pour boiling water over them. Press with paper towels to remove the surface oil. Cut into 1 inch (2.5 cm) squares.

2. Put the cut up tofu in a pan with the water, sugar and soy sauce and bring to a boil over medium heat. Turn the heat down to low and simmer for about 10 minutes. Leave to cool. Transfer to a storage container and refrigerate.

# Sweet & Sour Vegetables

**4 servings**

1 medium carrot, cut into batons
1 burdock root, cut into batons
  (optional)
Cornstarch, for dusting
Vegetable oil, for cooking
2 Tbsps sugar
1 Tbsp water
1 tsp rice vinegar
2 tsps soy sauce
White sesame seeds, to taste

1. Put the carrot and burdock in a plastic bag with cornstarch, and shake to coat. Shallow fry the batons, a few at a time, turning, until lightly browned and crispy. Drain.

2. Wipe the oil from the pan. Put in the sugar, water, vinegar and soy sauce and heat until bubbly. Put in the batons and mix to coat. Turn off the heat and sprinkle with sesame seeds. Cool, put in a storage container and refrigerate.

# Marinated Eggs

**4 servings**

4 eggs
½ cup (125 ml) water
Pinch of salt
1 Tbsp mirin
1 Tbsp soy sauce
1 small packet bonito flakes, optional

1. Let the eggs come to room temperature. Bring a generous amount of water to a boil in a pan. In a separate small pan make a marinade by bringing the ½ cup water, salt, mirin, soy sauce and bonito flakes to a boil. Allow to cool.

2. Put the eggs slowly into the boiling water. Boil for 7 mins. Drain and cool in cold water.

3. Peel the eggs and put into the marinade. Leave to marinate for at least half a day to absorb the flavors. Put into a storage container with the marinade, and refrigerate.

# Eggplant and Peppers in Ginger Sauce

**4 servings**

4 oz (100 g) eggplant
1 yellow bell pepper
1 piece grated ginger
1 tsp sugar
1½ Tbsps soy sauce
Vegetable oil, for cooking

1. Cut the eggplant into batons. Soak for a minute in a bowl of salted water. Drain, and pat dry with paper towels. Cut the bell pepper into ¾ inch (2 cm) squares. Mix the ginger, sugar and soy sauce in a bowl.

2. Heat the oil in a frying pan. Add the eggplant batons a few at a time, turning, until lightly browned. Put the hot batons in the marinade. Empty the oil from the pan and stir-fry the pepper. Mix the pepper into to the marinade. Leave to cool for 30 mins, put in a container and refrigerate.

## My Youngest Daughter Sue's bentos

It's been more than two years since my youngest daughter Sue started rebelling against me. When she was little she was so adorable, and the back seat of her mother's bicycle was reserved especially for her until she was quite big. She was the only one of my children to cling to me when we went out and say "I'm tired . . . I don't want to walk anymore . . . carry me piggyback, Mommy." At home, even when I was busy in the kitchen, if she felt neglected she'd come and beg to be picked up and hugged. (She is the baby, after all.) But now . . . these are the words that come out of that adorable mouth:

"Gross! Tacky!"

"Heh, you're getting fat."

Not cute at all. And although I don't have to make her a bento every day, on the days that I do, she never says anything nice about them to me. But the other day, an older girl that she looks up to in school, in her club, peeked inside Sue's bento box, and said "That looks sooo good!" The bento on that day happened to have one of Sue's favorites, a pan-fried pork patty. There were three precious patties, but she offered one to this girl that she adores so much. When Sue came home, she told me proudly that the girl had said "It's heavenly good!" When I replied "Ah, ok," without much emotion, she turned on me. "Wait a second! She said 'It's heavenly good'! That's awesome! Isn't it awesome? Why can't you be more excited?" she scolded me .

Oh, I got it . . .

Sue feels too awkward to thank her mother in her own words, so instead she is saying thank you while borrowing the words someone else has said.

Hmm. Maybe that awkwardness does remind me of someone . . .

# CHAPTER 3

# Tips for Good-Looking Bentos

If you want to get good reviews for your bentos from critical teenagers, especially girls, it's not enough that they simply taste good — the bentos have to look good too. In this chapter I'll give you some easy and foolproof tips.

Tip 1: Use multi-colored ingredients for beautiful bentos!
Tip 2: "Rice sandwiches" are tasty, good-looking and easy to make!
Tip 3: Serving something on top of rice makes a bento look delicious!

Ten tips for making your bentos look good.

This was sooo good!
Dangerously yummy!
A great bento!
—*My daughter Naa*

*Use multicolored ingredients for beautiful bentos!*

# Six-Color Soboro Rice-Bowl Bento

A soboro is a dish made with ground, diced, chopped or flaked meat, fish, egg, tofu or vegetables. Making a small amount of several kinds of soboro at the same time may seem like a lot of work, but if you use my method you can make this six-color soboro bento in just 10 minutes! Use the recipes on pages 80-81 to vary the soboro used too.

**1 serving for all recipes**

## Broccoli Soboro Ⓜ

6 broccoli florets
A pinch of bonito flakes
½ tsp soy sauce

## Eggplant Soboro Ⓜ

1 oz (30 g) eggplant, diced
2 tsps ponzu sauce
1 tsp sesame oil

## Potato Soboro Ⓜ

1 small potato, peeled and diced
1 tsp ground sesame seeds
Salt, to taste
1 tsp sesame oil

## Bell Pepper Soboro Ⓖ

¼ red bell pepper
Salt, to taste

## Curried Meat Soboro

½ cup (100 g) mixed ground beef and pork,
  or ground beef
Vegetable oil, for cooking
1 tsp mirin
1 tsp soy sauce
½ tsp curry powder

## Egg Soboro

1 egg, beaten with a pinch of salt
  and a pinch of sugar
Vegetable oil, for cooking

1. Cut the broccoli into small pieces. Rinse the potato pieces and drain. Wrap broccoli, eggplant and potato individually in cling film.

2. Dice the bell pepper and wrap in foil.

3. Put the cling film packets on a microwave-safe plate (photo 1) and microwave on high for 3 minutes. Put the foil packet under a preheated oven grill and cook for 3 minutes.

4. When cooked, mix each vegetable with the seasonings listed (photos 2 and 3). Let cool.

5. Stir-fry the meat until it changes color. Add the mirin, soy sauce and curry powder and stir-fry some more. Turn off the heat.

6. Heat some vegetable oil in a frying pan, pour in the egg mixture and make scrambled eggs. Take the eggs out of the pan.

7. Make a bed of rice in the bento box, and put the above items on top (see Photos 4 and 5).

*Basic instructions*

Wrap individually each item you'll be cooking in the microwave, and cook all at once.

When the microwaved vegetables are done, just open up the cling film and add the seasonings directly.

When the bell pepper is done cooking under the grill, open up the foil and add the seasonings directly onto it.

Spoon on the meat and egg. Use a fork for the vegetables. Leave a little in reserve to adjust the rows if needed.

Adjust the rows with the bits you have in reserve so that the surface of the bento is even.

My friends say my rice sandwiches look so cool! Please make them again for me, Mom!
—*My daughter Naa*

*"Rice sandwiches" are tasty, good-looking and easy to make from items in your stash!*

# Rice Sandwich Bento

An onigiri is a ball of rice that's formed into shape with your hands, a Japanese food that's been around for centuries. The rice sandwich – rice and various fillings wrapped in nori seaweed – is a relatively new phenomenon in Japan, but it's become a popular bento item. It's even captured the hearts of teenagers like my daughters. This one combines beef, carrot (or burdock root) and Japanese-style *tamagoyaki* rolled omelet to make a bento that looks great and is perfect for sharing.

## Rice Sandwiches

**Makes 2 sandwiches**

## Beef with Mustard

4 pieces thinly sliced beef, about 4 oz (100 g)
Vegetable oil, for cooking
1 tsp soy sauce
½ tsp karashi mustard or English mustard

## Tamagoyaki

2 eggs
Salt and sugar, to taste
Vegetable oil, for cooking
2 green shiso leaves
2 slices processed cheese

## Root Veg Stir-Fry

½ carrot, finely shredded (or ¼ burdock root)
Vegetable oil, for cooking
Handful bonito flakes, optional
½ tsp sugar
1 tsp mirin
2 Tbsps water
1 tsp soy sauce

## For the sandwich

2 bowls warm cooked rice
Salt, to taste
A little sesame oil
2 large sheets nori seaweed

* To make tamagoyaki in a regular frying pan, see page 90.

1. Cut the beef into bite-size pieces. Heat the oil in a frying pan, put in the beef in one layer and fry it on both sides until browned. Put on a plate and coat with the soy sauce and mustard.

2. Peel the carrot (or scrape the burdock root), rinse and drain. Stir-fry in a frying pan with some oil. When limp, add sugar, mirin, soy sauce and water. Cook, while stirring, until no moisture is left. Sprinkle in the bonito flakes and turn off the heat.

3. Mix the egg, salt and sugar in a bowl. Oil a tamagoyaki pan* and heat. Pour in half the egg mixture and cook until set on the bottom and still a bit wet on top. Fold in half and transfer to a plate. Repeat with the rest of the egg mixture. (Cut the edges of the cooked omelet pieces to fit the size of the rice sandwich.)

4. Add salt and sesame oil to the rice. Mix. Spread out a sheet of nori seaweed, and place ¼ of the rice in the middle (see Photo 1).

5. Top the rice with an omelet, 1 shiso leaf, a slice of cheese, half the carrot, and half the beef, in that order (see Photos 2 and 3). Top with another ¼ of the rice (see Photo 4) and wrap the nori seaweed around it (photos 5 and 6). Flip the rice sandwich over so the nori seaweed seams are facing down (see photo 7). When the nori has softened a little and adhered to the rice, cut the sandwich in half (see photo 8). Repeat to make 1 more sandwich.

### Assembly Instructions

Place ¼ of the rice on the rough side of the nori and shape into a square.

Put the omelet, shiso leaf, etc., on the rice in the order listed.

The cheese, carrot (or burdock root) and beef go on top.

Put another ¼ of the rice on top.

Fold in all 4 corners of the nori seaweed.

To make it neat, tuck in the folded corners of the nori.

Place the sandwich with the seams down, and leave to rest for a bit.

Cut the rice sandwich in half.

*To be used on top of rice or as rice sandwich fillings!*

# Fillings and Toppings for Rice

You can use these recipes as rice toppings, as rice sandwich fillings, or for onigiri rice-ball fillings too! It's really handy to keep a stock of these dishes ready to go.

## Salty Mushrooms Ⓜ

**1 serving**

Handful shimeji mushrooms, or mushrooms of your choice
Pinch of shio kombu or crazy salt
1 tsp mirin
1 tsp soy sauce

1. Trim and pull apart the mushrooms. Put everything in a microwave-safe container, cover with cling film and microwave on the high setting for 2 mins. Mix well to distribute the flavors.

## Eggplant and Tuna Soboro Ⓜ

**1 serving**

2 oz (50 g) eggplant, cubed
3 oz (75 g) canned tuna
Salt and pepper, to taste

1. Put the eggplant in a microwave-safe container and cover with cling film. Microwave on the high setting for 1½ minutes.

2. Add the drained tuna, salt and pepper and mix. Microwave for another 30 seconds.

## Buttery Beans Ⓜ

**1 serving**

10 green beans, trimmed
1 tsp butter
Pinch of shio kombu or crazy salt

1. Cut the green beans into 1 inch (2.5 cm) pieces. Put in a microwave-safe container, cover with cling film and microwave on the high setting for 1½ minutes.

2. Add the butter and shio kombu while still hot, and mix well.

## Sesame Carrots

**1 serving**

1 tsp sesame oil
1 medium carrot, in matchsticks
1 tsp mirin
1 tsp soy sauce
1 tsp white sesame seeds

1. Put the sesame oil and carrot into a frying pan and heat. Stir-fry until the carrot is limp. Add the mirin and soy sauce and stir-fry until there is no moisture left in the pan. Add the sesame seeds to finish.

## Scrambled Egg Ⓜ

**1 serving**

1 egg
½ tsp yukari salt or crazy salt
1 Tbsp mayo
½ tsp sugar

1. Break the egg into a microwave-safe cup. Add yukari, mayo and sugar, and beat well using a fork. Microwave on the high setting for 50–60 seconds. When the egg is cooked, break it up with a fork.

## Pepper Stir-Fry

**1 serving**

1 small bell pepper
1 tsp mayo
A little curry powder
Salt and pepper, to taste

1. Cut the bell pepper into thin strips.

2. Put the mayo and bell pepper in a frying pan and heat. Stir-fry until the bell pepper is limp, then add the curry powder, salt and pepper. Mix well.

## Chicken Soboro

**1 serving**

½ cup (100 g) ground chicken
1 Tbsp mirin
½ Tbsp soy sauce
½ tsp yuzu kosho, optional

1. Put chicken, mirin and soy sauce in a pan. Mix with a fork, breaking up any clumps. Turn on the heat and continue stirring until the meat is cooked.

2. Turn off the heat, add the yuzu kosho and mix well.

## Pork Soboro

**1 serving**

½ Tbsp sesame oil
½ cup (100 g) ground pork
½ Tbsp oyster sauce
½ Tbsp soy sauce
1 tsp sugar
½ tsp grated ginger

1. Heat the sesame oil in a frying pan. Add the pork and stir-fry.

2. When the meat changes color, add the oyster sauce, soy sauce, sugar and ginger. Continue cooking until there is no moisture left in the pan.

## Beef Soboro

**1 serving**

4 oz (100 g) thinly sliced beef
Vegetable oil, for cooking
1 tsp sugar
1 tsp sake
1 Tbsp ponzu sauce
1 umeboshi pickled plum, pitted
    and chopped into a paste

1. Cut the beef into thin strips. Heat the oil in a frying pan. Add the beef. Stir-fry briefly. When it changes color, add the other ingredients. Keep cooking until there is no moisture left in the pan.

## Mackerel Soboro

**2 servings**

7 oz (200 g) canned mackerel in
    water, drained
1 Tbsp sugar
1 Tbsp miso
1 tsp karashi or English mustard
1 tsp white sesame seeds

1. Put all ingredients in a small pan.

2. Cook, stirring occasionally, until there is no moisture left in the pan.

## Tofu Soboro

**1 serving**

5 oz (150 g) firm tofu, drained
1 Tbsp sesame oil
¼ tsp salt
1 small packet bonito flakes

1. Break the tofu into a small pan.

2. Add the oil to the pan. Turn on the heat. Stir-fry, while evaporating the moisture. Add the salt and bonito flakes, mix and turn off the heat.

## Celery Soboro Ⓜ

**1 serving**

½ celery stalk, thinly sliced
1 tsp sesame oil
1 tsp sugar
1 tsp miso
1 tsp mayo

1. Put the celery in a microwave-safe container, drizzle with sesame oil, cover with cling film and microwave on the high setting for 2 minutes.

2. Add sugar, miso and mayo, mix well and microwave for a further 30 seconds.

I can't get enough of the mayo flavor, Mom!
—*My daughter Naa*

*Serving something on a bed of rice always makes it look delicious!*

# Rice-Bowl Bentos

It's strange, but even the most mundane dishes look mouthwateringly good when served on top of a bed of plain rice. And if you can manage to get three different colors into your bento, it will look extra delicious! Try adding color using nori seaweed, shredded omelet, red pickled ginger, green shiso leaves and more!

## Salmon Rice-Bowl Bento

**1 serving**

4 oz (100 g) fresh salmon
Salt, to taste
1 tsp miso
1 tsp mayo
1 Tbsp chopped green onion (scallion)
Japanese seven spice, to taste
6 mild green chili peppers
Piece sweet potato, about 4 oz (100g)
1 serving cooked rice
2 Tbsps shredded nori seaweed

1. Cut the salmon in half, sprinkle with salt and leave to rest for about 10 minutes. Pat dry with paper towels.

2. Combine the miso, mayo, green onion and Japanese seven spice and spread on top of the salmon. Place the salmon on a piece of aluminum foil and place the chili peppers around it. (Do not close up the foil.)

3. Cut the sweet potato into batons and wrap in aluminum foil.

4. Grill both foil packets using a preheated oven or toaster oven for 7 to 8 minutes (see Photo 1). Open up the sweet potato packet while it's still hot and sprinkle with salt. Leave to cool.

5. Pack the rice into a bento box, sprinkle with nori seaweed and put the salmon, chili peppers and sweet potato on top (see Photos 2 to 4).

**Tips**

Cook everything at once using the grill.

Top the rice with nori seaweed, keeping the rice visible.

Place all the other food on top of the rice in an attractive way.

Show both the red skin and yellow inside of the potato to make the bento look pretty.

*Add freshness with green shiso leaves*

# Miso Pork Rice-Bowl Bento

**1 serving**
**1 tsp miso**
**1 tsp mirin**
**3 to 4 pieces thinly sliced pork,**
  **about 4 oz (100 g)**
**1 egg**
**A little salt**
**A little sugar**
**Vegetable oil, for cooking**
**3 green shiso leaves**
**1 serving cooked rice**

1. Mix the miso and mirin together and spread it evenly over the meat slices. Wrap in cling film and refrigerate overnight.

2. Break the egg into a bowl, add a little salt and sugar and beat well.

3. Heat up some vegetable oil in a frying pan. Pour in the egg mixture and make a thin omelet. Turn it over once and cook the other side quickly. Take it out, cool and shred thinly.

4. Put the miso-marinated pork into the empty frying pan. Cook over low heat on both sides, being careful not to let it burn.

5. Fill a bento box with the rice and top with the shredded omelet. Alternate slices of pork and shiso leaves on top of the egg and rice.

* If using very thinly sliced pork, use 4 slices instead of 3 as shown.

*The sweet-salty flavors of the vegetables really whet your appetite*

# Sweet and Savory Eggplant and Tofu Rice-Bowl Bento

**1 serving**
2 oz (50 g) eggplant
½ abura-age tofu pouch
3 tablespoons water
1 Tbsp mirin
A little sugar
1 tsp soy sauce
1 egg
Pinch each of salt and sugar
Vegetable oil, for cooking
1 serving cooked rice
Sugar snap pea, for garnish
Beni shoga red pickled ginger, or
    sweet pickles, for garnish

1. Cut the eggplant into 1 inch (2.5 cm) dice. Soak the eggplant pieces briefly in a bowl of salted water and drain. Pat dry with paper towels. Cut the tofu into 1 inch (2.5 cm) dice.

2. Put the eggplant, tofu, 3 tablespoons of water, mirin, sugar and soy sauce into a small pan. Cook while stirring occasionally until there is no moisture left.

3. Break the egg into a bowl and beat well with salt and sugar. Heat up some vegetable oil in a frying pan, pour in the egg mixture and scramble it.

4. Pack the rice into a bento box and top with the scrambled egg, then the eggplant-tofu mix. Microwave the snap pea for about 10 seconds and place on top, along with some shredded beni shoga.

# Ten Tips for Making Your Bentos Look Good

Even on days when the bento you're making doesn't look very appetizing, don't give up. With a few tricks up your sleeve, you can transform the most ordinary bento into something pretty, just by following these ten simple tips!

## 1 Cherry tomatoes aren't the only red food! Here are some other red food items that can perk up a dull looking bento.

For those times when you feel that something red would perk up your bento, but you don't have any cherry tomatoes or red bell peppers, try having some beni shoga (red pickled ginger) and umeboshi pickled plums in stock. In addition, red seasoning ingredients like yukari shiso salt (available at your Japanese grocery) or ketchup can add a bright red accent to your bentos.

beni shoga (red pickled ginger)

umeboshi pickled plums

food cooked with ketchup

yukari (red shiso leaf salt)

## 2 When you don't have any red food on hand, perk up your bento by using a red bento box or red bento cups!

If you have a bento box that is red on the inside, like a lacquered box, or if you have red cup liners on hand, your bento will look more colorful even if the food isn't.

## 3 Everything looks good when wrapped in an omelet.

The rolled omelet known as tamagoyaki is a classic bento item (see page 90). If you have something left over from last night's dinner, but it's pretty brown, you can use it as a filling inside a rolled omelet. If the filling is on the salty side, make the egg mixture a little sweet by adding sugar, to balance out the flavors.

86

# 4 Make the most of decorative paper.

You can find decorative food-safe cooking paper for sale online and at kitchen-supply and party-supply stores. Use these pretty papers in your bentos and even if the food is brown and plain, it will instantly look much prettier, especially if the paper has some red in it. Take care to choose sturdy paper—cheap paper may tear when it absorbs moisture.

There are many different kinds of decorative cooking paper.

Crumple up a piece of paper.

Spread it out and line the bento box with it.

Arrange the food on the paper.

Done! The paper frames the food and makes it look pretty.

# 5 Keep some polka-dot food items in stock for instant prettiness.

Round "polka dot" foods used as toppings and garnishes will, like magic, make bentos look pretty. For example, use bright green edamame beans or yellow corn kernels and scatter them on top of your bentos to make them come to life. Sugar snap peas, with the peas still in the pods, look beautiful. Make the most of these naturally cute foods!

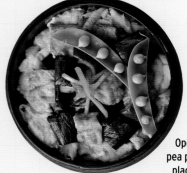

Open sugar snap pea pods look pretty placed on top of a bento!

sugar snap peas

frozen shelled edamame beans

frozen corn kernels

## 6 Decorate the top of the rice.

Even if the rest of the bento is hopelessly plain looking, you can still decorate the rice. Try placing small pickled plums in a regular pattern on top, or making a pickled plum into a heart shape. Or how about using some colorful rice sprinkles? Think of the rice as a plain white canvas, to decorate with your own food art.

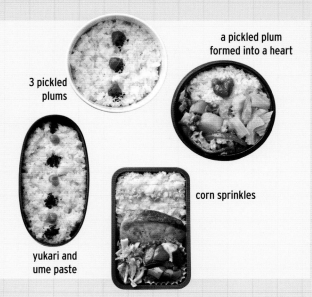

3 pickled plums

a pickled plum formed into a heart

corn sprinkles

yukari and ume paste

## 7 Use a bento box with a domed lid to stop the contents getting squished.

Even if the bento looks great when you pack it, too often the contents get squished when you close the lid—which isn't going to get rave reviews from your kids! Try a bento box with a domed lid. Even if you pile the food high in the box, the domed space means nothing gets squished and the contents stay looking attractive. This type of bento box is especially useful when you are making "on top of rice" bentos.

Try a bento box with a domed lid . . .

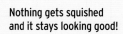

Nothing gets squished and it stays looking good!

## 8 For a change of pace, include a pretty disposable fork with the bento box!

Teenage girls love things that remind them of cute cafes. Even if the contents of the bento don't look that pretty or elegant, you can add a bit of "cafe style" by including a stylish utensil, such as a disposable wooden fork. Just stick it onto the bento box with a piece of colorful washi tape, for a trendy touch that your daughters will love!

Tape a disposable fork on top of a bento box.

## 9 Make original food picks using washi tape.

Food picks often feel either too childish or too grownup to appeal to teenagers. So I often make my own, using washi tape or decorative masking tape. Wrap the blunt end of a toothpick with washi tape, and cut the tape to leave a flag shape about ½ inch (1 cm) long. Voilà, you have a very cute handmade pick. (Be sure the tape you use is very clean to keep the food from spoiling.)

## 10 Use washi tape as cute rice-ball labels!

Even a simple onigiri rice-ball bento can be made pretty with just a little effort. Wrap the rice balls in cling film, write the flavor on a piece of washi tape (use one that you can write on easily) and stick it on the cling film. Not only does it look cute, it makes identifying the contents of the rice ball a snap. Kids always appreciate little touches like this.

**Washi tape can be used in all sorts of ways in bentos!**

**Make it easy to identify the filling.**

# Making Rolled Omelets in a Regular Frying Pan

The rolled omelet known as tamagoyaki is a common bento-box item in Japan, and appears in several recipes in this book. The small, rectangular frying pan used to make tamagoyaki is an everyday utensil in the Japanese kitchen. These frying pans are fairly inexpensive and readily available online, but if you don't have one, it's possible to make tamagoyaki in a regular, round frying pan, by folding the omelet into layers rather than rolling it. This method produces tamagoyaki that is thinner, with fewer layers than one made in a tamagoyaki pan, but it will still be great!

Use a small, 6 inch (15 cm) diameter pan, preferably with a nonstick surface.

1. Mix the eggs and seasonings and any other ingredients to be included in the tamagoyaki mixture as instructed in the recipe. In the meantime, spread oil in the small frying pan and heat over medium heat.

2. Test to see if the pan is hot enough by putting in a few drops of the egg mixture. If the egg sets immediately the pan is ready. If the pan is smoking, it's too hot, so cool it for a bit before proceeding.

3. Pour in the egg mixture, and stir gently with a fork until it's half set.

4. Working quickly, fold one third of the egg over with a spatula.

5. Fold the other third over with the spatula. It should now look like a regular omelet.

6. Fold over one third of one of the narrow ends of the omelet and press it down with the spatula.

7. Fold the other narrow end of the omelet and press down again. You should have a small, square omelet. Flip the square over and press down one more time to ensure it's cooked through. Take out of the pan and cool down slightly before cutting in half.

Recipe courtesy of Makiko Itoh, a bilingual writer specializing in Japanese food and culture. She is the author of the bestselling *Just Bento Cookbook* and its sequel, *The Just Bento Cookbook 2* (both Kodansha International), and the owner of several websites dedicated to Japanese culture, including JustBento.com. She is also the translator of this book.

# Index of Main Ingredients

# "Books to Span the East and West"

**Tuttle Publishing** was founded in 1832 in the small New England town of Rutland, Vermont (USA). Our core values remain as strong today as they were then—to publish best-in-class books which bring people together one page at a time. In 1948, we established a publishing outpost in Japan—and Tuttle is now a leader in publishing English-language books about the arts, languages and cultures of Asia. The world has become a much smaller place today and Asia's economic and cultural influence has grown. Yet the need for meaningful dialogue and information about this diverse region has never been greater. Over the past seven decades, Tuttle has published thousands of books on subjects ranging from martial arts and paper crafts to language learning and literature—and our talented authors, illustrators, designers and photographers have won many prestigious awards. We welcome you to explore the wealth of information available on Asia at **www.tuttlepublishing.com.**

Published by Tuttle Publishing, an imprint of Periplus Editions (HK) Ltd.

**www.tuttlepublishing.com**

ISBN 978-4-8053-1577-4

Tenkichi Kaachan no Asa 10-pun, Arumono dakede Homerare Bento by INOUE Kanae
Copyright ©2015 INOUE Kanae
All rights reserved.
Original Japanese edition published by Bungeishunju Ltd., Japan in 2105.
World English translation rights reserved by Tuttle Publishing, under the license granted by INOUE Kanae, Japan, arranged with Bungeishunju Ltd., Japan through Japan Uni Agency, Inc., Japan.

English translation ©2020 Periplus Editions (HK) Ltd.
English translation by Makiko Itoh.

Book jacket background texture from MediaLoot.com

Distributed by:
**North America, Latin America & Europe**
Tuttle Publishing
364 Innovation Drive, North Clarendon
VT 05759-9436 U.S.A.
Tel: 1 (802) 773-8930; Fax: 1 (802) 773-6993
info@tuttlepublishing.com
www.tuttlepublishing.com

**Japan**
Tuttle Publishing
Yaekari Building 3rd Floor
5-4-12 Osaki Shinagawa-ku, Tokyo 141 0032
Tel: (81) 3 5437-0171; Fax: (81) 3 5437-0755
sales@tuttle.cop; wwwtuttleco.jp

**Asia Pacific**
Berkeley Books Pte. Ltd.
3 Kallag Sector, #04-01, Singapore 349278
Tel: (65) 67412178; Fax: (65) 67412179
inquiries@periplus.com.sg
www.tuttlepublishing.com

Printed in China    2312EP

26 25 24 23        10 9 8 7 6 5 4 3